A Phone Call to the Future

A Phone Call to the Future

New and Selected Poems

MARY JO SALTER

Alfred A. Knopf   *New York*   2008

Some poems in this collection originally appeared in the following works:
Henry Purcell in Japan, copyright © 1984 by Mary Jo Salter (Alfred A. Knopf)
Unfinished Painting, copyright © 1989 by Mary Jo Salter (Alfred A. Knopf)
Sunday Skaters, copyright © 1994 by Mary Jo Salter (Alfred A. Knopf)
A Kiss in Space, copyright © 1999 by Mary Jo Salter (Alfred A. Knopf)
Open Shutters, copyright © 2003 by Mary Jo Salter (Alfred A. Knopf)

For information on where the remaining poems have previously appeared,
please see the acknowledgments.

Library of Congress Cataloging-in-Publication Data
Salter, Mary Jo.
A phone call to the future : new and selected poems / by Mary Jo Salter.—1st ed.
p. cm.
ISBN 978-0-307-26718-4
I. Title.
PS3569.A46224P49 2008
811'.54—dc22
2007041105

So many friends to thank.
Especially you:

Daniel Hall
Fred Hersch
Ann Hulbert
Cynthia Zarin

Contents

FROM *Sunday Skaters* (1994)

FROM *A Kiss in Space* (1999)

NEW POEMS

WAKE-UP CALL

The water is slapping *wake up, wake up,* against the boat
chugging away from Venice, infinite essence
of what must end because it is beautiful,

Venice that shrinks to a bobbing, pungent postcard
and then to nothing at all as the automatic
doors at the airport obligingly shut behind you.

Re-enter a world where everything's much the same,
where you've gone slack again, and don't even know it,
so unaware that you actually shrug to yourself,

I'll be back, and yes, for some lucky stiffs it's true,
sometimes it's you, you're sure to get more chances
at Venice, and Paris, and that blessed, unmarked place

where you sat on a bench and he kissed you that first time,
so many kisses, you hoped he would never stop,
you can hope, at least, not ever to forget it,

or forget how your babies, latching onto your breast,
would roll up their eyes in an ecstasy that was comic
in its seriousness, though your joy was no less grave,

but you're not going back to so much, and more and more,
the longer you live there's more not to go back to,
and what you demand in your gratitude and greed

is more life in which to get so attached to something,
someone or someplace, you're sure you'll die right then
when you can't have it back, something you don't even know

the name of yet, but will be yours before receding
as an indispensable ache; what you're saying
is *Lord, surprise me with even more to miss.*

FRIDAY HARBOR, 10 A.M.

In the distance, grand
as an open-air showroom
of upended pianos,

a flotilla of yachts:
each a church equipped
with a spar for steeple,

or a high-tech antenna
tuned in to money,
the favored station.

Still, now there's static
on the harbor channel,
a sputter of rain

speckling the water,
and under the oddly
sunny cloud-cover

the Sound breaks in scallops,
as wave overlaps
with shoreward wave,

carves itself into what
appears is a pebbly
black-and-white woodcut,

on which somebody, all wet,
all elbows, is rowing
his rowboat in like a robot.

LUNAR ECLIPSE
in memory of Anthony Hecht

Days after you died,
when your face was everywhere
I turned (craggy, inclined

to be reflective, kindly, in
parentheses of pure
white hair and white goatee),

a lunar eclipse, the last
we'd see for years, was promised,
and I took a kitchen chair,

a pencil, and a notebook
out to the moonstruck driveway,
knowing you'd be there.

A shadow-boxer's blow
had caught the moon's left jaw;
in silence and slow motion

it crept up, a gloved fist
of darkness that kept looming.
In saddened admiration

I watched the giant fail—
a dimming, a diminution,
among the attendant stars.

Dark poet, you were called.
Your last poems were in keeping
with that judgment; gave a world

where "no joy goes unwept."
Yet the act of making
was light and lightness still

when a man of eighty-one
immortalized the sun
on his wife's face as she slept.

I stayed out late, in hope
such clear skies would provide
a luminary's comeback,

a rematch with itself.
And friends told me they saw it.
As for our moon, a sudden

cloud—a blanket pulled
over the vanquished head
of one on his deathbed—

was my signal to go in.
Not enough light to write by.
Later, I would try.

COSTANZA BONARELLI

A bust that looks just-kissed,
  from the blind intensity
of her gaze to the somewhat swollen
  parted lips, to the parting,
    above her rumpled chemise,
of two soft breasts his hands
  lifted from stone, Bernini's

    lover was designed
  to please—to have and hold
in his own eyes as forever
  undone and to-be-done-to,
    a melting readiness.
Oh the inconstant Costanza,
  true-to-life but untrue!—

    whose drawing power, coiled
  as the heavy braid he pulled
behind her head, yet loose
  as the involving tendrils
    that tumbled to one side,
originated from
  within a designing woman.

    If either alone suffices
  (love or art, that is)
to lead a man to believe
  whole days can be best spent
    lost in a woman's hair,
how could he not have wept
  at the upswept and downfallen

tresses of one who was
both singular ideal—
a thing he'd hewn from rock
into his own landmark
in portraiture, quintessence
of the sinuous baroque—
and all too two-faced mistress?

That she was capable
of deception—this was fine,
one guesses: a frisson
at first, that she (the wife
of his apprentice) gave
in private no resistance
to a greater man's assistance.

But now the great man's brother?
His brother? When the rumor
reached him, Bernini sent
a razor-bearing servant
to do what must be done.
He wasn't going to kill her.
No, but he'd leave a scar,

a sort of *Kilroy was here;*
he'd affix his stamp, he'd fix her
once and for all, for good—
indeed, he'd have his thug
underling slash her face,
her living flesh, with a tool
not so unlike the one

that he alone, the master,
had been skilled enough to wield,
watching the marble yield
to each sweet, painstaking stroke
of chisel against cheek
until, so real, she fairly
cried out for more.

SONG OF THE CHILDREN
April 2005

Two years since the spring
of the invasion, a well-conducted
symphony of fireworks on the screen,
I sit at home, half-humming
a tune from miles away inside my brain.
I think I know, at least, the song's refrain—
In the end it's about the children
In the end it's about the children—
What's wrong with me? The music isn't coming.

"What is the grass?" the child asked Whitman,
gathering strangeness in his outstretched palms.
"All flesh is grass," said Brahms
in well-aimed thunder, merciless and grand.
What is this hook
the child is left with, he who lost
two parents, and a sister, and a hand?
Who bears the cost?
How can I tell him—I who can barely look?

A shrug then: fate is fickle;
so many soldiers won't be getting older;
as another year's worth of recruits
hoists its rifles, shoulder to young shoulder,
another pen rests on my ink-stained knuckle.
I have been spared, it seems, for another year
to compose the awkward rags of my regrets—
In the end it's about the children
In the end it's about the children—

Another year has curled
in on itself;
under the wheels of Humvees caked
with dust, the turning, half-cocked world
is skewered on its axis.
My pen is angled too—is glad enough
to bleed into long ranks and files of taxes:
before my country's army rolling forward
I write my check, the white flag of a coward.

BEACH HOUSE, SPACE-TIME

Slung from the ceiling,
fishnetting from the Fifties
sags from exposed beam to beam,
each swag with a hefty
conch inside it
curled like a sailor
dozing in a hammock.

A weekend guest, flat-backed
on the couch, has just awakened.
First hint of light.
Four-something in the morning,
and for once she isn't worrying
about work, or about whether
without sleep her day is shot.

Oddly, it makes her happy
that the light fixture up there
looks like the rolling pin
in the kitchen,
where cobwebs that connect
the short, salt-heavy curtains
to the walls went unremarked

all through a dinner of corn
on the cob (each one, she thinks,
a little rolling pin),
green beans and, in a delicious
slapdash marinade
(never to be repeated;
made of what they had),

fresh haddock from the grill.
She asks herself if "haddock"
would ever, at some other
hour than four, or somewhere
else—she means back home—
have wound up in a rhyme
with "hammock."

And what does *that* signify?
Above her head,
her lightest thoughts are weights
caught in the net, along
with the single lobster claw,
the starfish like a splay
body on the beach,

some comet-tailed crustaceans—
like textbook illustrations
of how, when you drop planets
into the accepting
maw of the universe,
its ready-made graph paper
that accounts for gravity

dips with curved space-time.
Or so it seems to one
whose position on the couch,
Einstein would insist,
is as good a place to start
as the stars, or the heads of people
still asleep upstairs.

POINT OF VIEW

As if the leaden clouds
   had let loose all their force
      as sharpened pencils,

the rain falls into line—
   or dotted lines, in length
      and slant so uniform,

so steadily dashed off,
   they are themselves the calm
      within the storm.

They take mathematical
   pleasure, it appears,
      hatching plane on plane

(vertically propped,
   transparent, infinite,
      on that plot of grass),

and seem to come from some
   old hand at this, the same
      cartoonist who

indicates a pane
   of glass, first, with a square,
      then two or three

forty-five-degree-
   angled strokes that fall
      within it, parallel

vectors of the glare
glinting off this window
which, like the sun today,

is otherwise not merely
not thought of, but (for our
purposes) not there.

"GERANIUMS BEFORE BLUE MOUNTAIN"

August Macke, 1911

How trusting the hand that balanced them
on the railing of a farmhouse porch—
    three terra cotta pots
of geraniums that a careless elbow
    could send to smithereens.

But was it the farmer or the artist
(naïf or faux-naïf, or neither)
    who slid two of the plants a bit
to the left, one to the right, creating
    a gap through which to view

another farmhouse in the middle
distance, in two shades of blue,
    with childish chimney smoke
billowing domestic joy
    so high it seems volcanic?

. . . Seems rightly to belong, in fact,
to the mountain whose blue mass
    in the background, pitched
itself like a slate-roofed, sagging house,
    demands most of the canvas.

Whoever first had set the scene—
who placed the geraniums "before,"
    as the translation has it,
the mountain, and made the flowers loom,
    upstaging all the rest—

what's clear is that somebody meant,
like us, to overwhelm the sublime
    with a pint-sized ornament
that was human; to get the fingers dirty
    in setting things just right.

August Macke, then twenty-four,
may well have been too fresh-faced not
    to paint the scarlet, pert
geraniums largely as they were.
    Or that's the background story,

learned after I had left the museum
and typed his name: there on the screen
    bloomed images of heads,
bright-hued but faceless, which he'd become
    a little famous for;

and ladies in parrot-jackets who stand,
behatted and parasoled, peering in shop
    windows for more hats;
zoo parrots; a newspaper reader
    hunched on a park bench;

the artist's wife with a plate of apples;
sun-yellow cafés. "Unlike his fellow
    German Expressionists,"
a critic wrote, "he was known to salute
    the primacy of life."

Known after 1914—when,
leaving in Bonn the wife and children,
   in a French village he met
a bullet, and dropped there in his trench
   facedown, like a flowerpot.

GOODBYE, TRAIN

I'm stepping off the train behind a pair
of thirtysomethings with their baby daughter.

The father will stay fit for years, I think,
though here and there, his hair's a little thin;

the mother's confident in new blue jeans
she knows are sexy—but carefully, tastefully so.

Seeing them floods me at once—I can't say why—
with solicitude. Delight, and envy. Pain.

"Goodbye, train," the mother says, and then,
"Say 'goodbye, train,' 'bye bye.' " She waves her hand

theatrically, the way we often will
with children, so that nobody can find us

guilty, ourselves, of any silliness—
of joy in the trainman's cap, his ticket-punch.

The little girl is propped on her father's hip
and pointing vaguely at a world of things

she's just come to know, and which now must go away.
How grave she seems!—a toothless oracle.

I see too how I look, if anyone's looking:
a weathered niceness, a trudging competence.

That's how I follow, twenty years ahead
of the parents, as I lug my bags behind them,

vowing to keep a stranger's proper distance—
as I did from those two lovesick teenagers

clinging in tears some stations back, when he
prepared himself to be left there on the platform

by a girl who swore it wasn't possible,
and both were stunned to discover that it was.

I think what luck it is, to be one who says
goodbye to trains instead of other people.

MUSICAL CHAIR

At the behest of our hostess, the senior member
of the dinner party, everyone takes a chair
out to the lawn. No sitting this game out.
The final wedge of watermelon dispensed with,
necks and ankles sprayed with bug repellent,
we're sticky in every particular, hair silted
and still half-wet from long swims in the pond
that has begun to take on the purplish drama
of the sky where clouds, pure white and lightly shaped—
such sun-buffed edges, spaced with such offhand
perfection of proportion—an hour ago
had been floating, expressionless, in shallow blue.
Syncopations of cloud, like not-quite-random
drops in the pond's bottom, sudden to someone
happening on a deep spot. "Oh! It's cold!"
had been the repeated cry, a call to laughter—
complaint, like all else today, a luxury
assumed in the general clemency of June.
Lappings at the dock more clocklike now,
the water's flatter, no longer being displaced
by some who clambered, swaying, out of kayaks,
or swimmers large and small who hauled themselves
upward to waiting hands and a promised meal—
seasonal, plentiful—that has ended. Everything
has an end.

And this is how such evenings at her house
have always ended: with a game from nursery school.
In this is infinity, or so it feels
when we arrange the roundup of old chairs
as variously faulty as our bodies:
a ladderback, a rocker, a leatherette

swivelly thing, four folding chairs dismissed
from their ceremonial posts around the card
table that serves, instead, to pose a puzzle
forever on the brink of being solved
but never quite.

Somebody has located the boom box
and tuned it to the golden oldies station
which, for the moment, is aimless talk and static.
"Music!" decrees our hostess (her generation
registers none of it as truly old).
It's the big bang: a crowd of planets startle,
clown and falter, then orbit in a steady,
blasé ellipse before opinion splits—
some of us dawdling, others speeding up—
as to which course would save you, should the cosmos
come to a halt.

"Pete! Pete!" The youngest one, just three, with help
from several coaches, scrambles to stake out
the wicker doll-chair (which nearly no one else
could have taken without breaking). "Good job, Pete!"
Fireplug-solemn, he claims a Ptolemaic
certainty that the earth—himself—is central.
This is his throne. It takes a few more songs,
a few more seats removed, before we gather
that now he chooses not to make the circuit,
hovering, instead, with little hops,
near territory first seized as his own;
and by the fourth cut, fifth, he gives up all
pretense of rising from his right position.
He, who any actuary would pronounce

likely to have the longest time to live
of any of us, is the most conservative.
His mother nudges, tells him to be polite
to the other children. "Come on, Pete, let's dance—"
But he won't budge. His feet pinned to the ground,
he looks down from the hill to where he swam
today, in a pond now deepening to a shade
that looks like bedtime, that looks like the dark place
you hide in under the covers, when afternoon—
such a happy, happy one—is gone, and he
will not be unseated.

EXECUTIVE SHOESHINE

It may go on snowing forever,
but meanwhile, how he's basking
in the sun of his own multitasking!
He's perched erect on his throne
looking down on the airport food court,
as the silver snail of a cell phone
earpiece hooked to his ear
hangs on his every word.
No way to cut him short
until the runways are cleared
and they've finished out there de-icing
the right wing, then the left wing
of all those planes before his.
Could he strike us a deal with the weather?
The man hunched below him polishes
one wingtip, then the other.

PICKET FENCE WITH PEACOCK

Only from that approach—
  from our errant angle as
    we walked around the park—
      and only at that moment
      would we have been likely,
  between two slats, to spy

beyond a high picket fence
  the peacock. Seeming to think
    himself alone, he stood
      stiffly and long in the Dutch
    ruff of himself, the tall
  pleats behind his head

narrowly refusing
  deployment until, for no
    discernable cause, he turned
      to us (who were peeking silently;
      never speak first to royalty)
  and, with a Chaplinesque

self-possession, rocked
  from side to side, as if drunk,
    before flinging his coat wide
      to expose nothing (although this
    was something) but its lining
  of open, long-lashed eyes.

A flasher who'd arrest
  instead of being arrested.
    A cardsharp who could put
      himself away like a hand.

We showed off, too, for a bit—
turned faceup all our words

within words for the gaudy,
    ungainly, poker-faced
        peacock who kept strutting
        in the yard as his own fan.
        We knew, as we walked on,
        the fence behind was shutting.

POETRY SLALOM

Much less
the slam
than the slalom
gives me a thrill:
that solemn, no-fuss
Olympian skill
in skirting flag after flag
of the bloody obvious;
the fractional
lag,
while speeding downhill,
at the key
moment,
in a sort of whole-
body trill:
the note repeated,
but elaborated,
more touching and more
elevated
for seeming the thing
to be evaded.

ROSES AND MONA LISA

Long-settled, it seemed, by the time I came to
sit across from them, the boy and his mother
(I assumed she was his mother, and not an
aunt or a nanny)

were wedged in for the baking ride to Brooklyn.
He, elbows held close, was riveted to a
video game of some sort; she was lifting
(was that the title?

yes, so it was: *Mona Lisa*) a thin but
hardback art book so near her nose I barely
caught a glimpse of her face (did she know she
needed new glasses?)

and, for minutes, her whole head was replaced by
the one on the cover; but now and then she'd
bring the book down a notch, to watch her feet shift,
balancing roses

stuffed, too tall a bouquet, into the shopping
bag propped between her knees, which went on pitching
sideways each time the train would round a bend;
when she leaned forward

you could see how intent she was on keeping
the roses upright and fresh, without somehow
losing her precious minutes left for reading.
Who would have thought it

(I thought) that, snaggle-toothed and dressed so badly,
she would insist upon her daily ration
of beauty in nature, or in a painter's
picturing nature—

ashamed, of course, that I'd think that; I nearly
wish, or I wish I did, that the punishment
coming could have been leveled at me instead.
Having succeeded

now at his miniature game, the boy turned to
tell her about it; nudged her for attention
just when, her roses straight again, she'd ventured
back to the painting.

Raising her arm, but not her gaze, she whacked him
hard on the mouth. In time a mysterious
smile had crept over him, almost as if he'd
grown to expect it.

AURORA BOREALIS

An arc of searchlight
and, as such, a not quite
accurate
way of going about it:

if you were looking
for some lost thing
in the ring
of dark circling

the earth,
if the path
of light you hunted with
(emerging from underneath

the horizon, and trained
not by you but a hand
unseen) ended
with a sideways bend,

if its torch forked
and flickered
as if overworked,
if it torqued

inside itself with a wow
and a flutter, a now
you see it now
you don't, how

long would it take
before you'd make
the leap?—Would you look
at those freak

streaks in the sky
forever before saying, "I
see the light:
this *is* what I sought tonight"?

PLEASE FORWARD

A yellowed paperback
so brittle that each page
snaps out when I turn it—
well, it ought to last me
through this little flight

of fancy in a prop plane,
a throwback to my childhood.
Have I even tried
Peer Gynt before? Not sure.
You reach an age when classics

are what you *must* have read.
Certainly there can't be
any worse translation
than this one; and no tale
of trolls should ever call

for footnotes this pedantic.
Munching peanuts, bored,
how could I have missed
till now (tucked in at page
sixteen) the fusty postcard

addressed to "Mrs. Gert
Ferrie"? (Yes, as if
she too were supernatural.)
And look, a cryptic message
which, though uncompelling

as the book it's slipped into,
seems, somehow, more telling
just for landing here:
"Well how did things go?
I hope alright,"

is how Gert's correspondent,
name illegible,
begins; and ends, "we spent
a lot of time in the rain.
Take care and God bless."

Ah, I see . . . So Gert,
some forty years ago,
had sat there in Milwaukee
and tried to read this book,
had failed, like me, and stuck

the postcard in the early
scene where she got stuck.
And worrying, probably,
about a host of "things"
that hadn't gone "alright,"

she hadn't gazed for long
at this photo of "The Great
North Door, Singing Tower,
Mountain Lake Sanctuary,
Lake Wales, Florida,"

an icy Technicolor-
bluish stone façade
in which a golden door—
with pictures in each panel,
like stories cut and pasted

from a grander drama
time had hammered out—
seems to be the entrance
to the Hall of the Mountain King . . .
A dream door, to more visions

lacking a master builder;
to mysteries half-banal,
half-magical, we happen
upon: as when, today,
a dog-eared traveler

myself, I slipped into
a used bookstore (seduced
by time-warped, slovenly
volumes left to lean on
the most specious of connections),

and as if from a mail slot
in my own door, I took
in hand this paperback—
which now, before we land,
I slip into the pocket

behind a stranger's seat.

SOMEBODY ELSE'S BABY

From now on they always are, for years now
they always have been, but from now on you know
they are, they always will be,

from now on when they cry and you say
wryly to their mother, *better you than me,*
you'd better mean it, you'd better

hand over what you can't have, and graciously.

A PHONE CALL TO THE FUTURE

I.

Who says science fiction
is only set in the future?
After a while, the story that looks least
believable is the past.
The console television with three channels.
Black-and-white picture. Manual controls:
the dial clicks when you turn it, like the oven.
You have to get up and walk somewhere to change things.
You have to leave the house to mail a letter.

Waiting for letters. The phone rings: you're not there.
You'll never know. The phone rings, and you are,
there's only one, you have to stand or sit
plugged into it, a cord
confines you to the room where everyone
is also having dinner.
Hang up the phone. The family's having dinner.

Waiting for dinner. You bake things in the oven.
Or Mother does. That's how it always is.
She sets the temperature: it takes an hour.

The patience of the past.
The typewriter forgives its own mistakes.
You type on top sheet, carbon, onion skin.
The third is yours, a record of typeovers,
clotted and homemade-looking, like the seams
on dresses cut out on the dining table.
The sewing machine. The wanting to look nice.
Girls who made their dresses for the dance.

2.
This was the Fifties: as far back as I go.
Some of it lasted decades.
That's why I remember it so clearly.

Also because, as I lie in a motel room
sometime in 2004, scrolling
through seventy-seven channels on my back
(there ought to be more—this is a cheap motel room),
I can revisit evidence, hear it ringing.
My life is movies, and tells itself in phones.

The rotary phone, so dangerously languid
and loud when the invalid must dial the police.
The killer coming up the stairs can hear it.
The detective ducks into a handy phone booth
to call his sidekick. Now at least there's touch tone.
But wait, the killer's waiting in the booth
to try to strangle him with the handy cord.
The cordless phone, first noted in the crook
of the neck of the secretary
as she pulls life-saving files.
Files come in drawers, not in the computer.
Then funny computers, big and slow as ovens.
Now the reporter's running with a cell phone
larger than his head,
if you count the antenna.

They're Martians, all of these people,
perhaps the strangest being the most recent.
I bought that phone. I thought it was so modern.

Phones shrinking year by year, as stealthily
as children growing.

3.
It's the end of the world.
Or people are managing, after the conflagration.
After the epidemic. The global thaw.
Everyone's stunned. Nobody combs his hair.
Or it's a century later, and although
New York is gone, and love, and everyone
is a robot or a clone, or some combination,

you have to admire the technology of the future.
When you want to call somebody, you just think it.
Your dreams are filmed. Without a camera.
You can scroll through the actual things that happened,
and nobody disagrees. No memory.
No point of view. None of it necessary.

Past the time when the standard thing to say
is that, no matter what, the human endures.
That whatever humans make of themselves
is therefore human.
Past the transitional time
when humanity as we know it was there to say that.
Past the time we meant well but were wrong.
It's less than that, not anymore a concept.
Past the time when mourning was a concept.

Of course, such a projection,
however much I believe it, is sentimental—

belief being sentimental.
The thought of a woman born
in the fictional Fifties.

That's what I mean. We were Martians. Nothing's stranger
than our patience, our humanity, inhumanity.
Our worrying about robots. Earplug cell phones
that make us seem to be walking about like loonies
talking to ourselves. Perhaps we are.

All of it was so quaint. And I was there.
Poetry was there; we tried to write it.

Henry Purcell in Japan

(1985)

REFRAIN

But let his disposition have that scope
As dotage gives it.

— GONERIL TO ALBANY

Never afflict yourself to know the cause,
said Goneril, her mind already set.
No one can tell us who her mother was

or, knowing, could account then by the laws
of nurture for so false and hard a heart.
Never afflict yourself to know the cause

of Lear's undoing: if without a pause
he shunned Cordelia, as soon he saw the fault.
No one can tell us who her mother was,

but here's a pretty reason seven stars
are seven stars: because they are not eight.
Never afflict yourself to know the cause—

like servants, even one's superfluous.
The King makes a good fool: the Fool is right.
No one can tell him who his mother was

when woman's water-drops are all he has
against the storm, and daughters cast him out.
Never afflict yourself to know the cause;
no one can tell you who your mother was.

AT CITY HALL

"What kind of license you looking for?"
the woman lounging behind
the counter asked. What *kind*?
A question so disarming the groom

(just outvoicing the dusty carriage
wheels of ceiling fans)
conceded ignorance. "Don't mind
him," the bride said. "A marriage

license." Across the room,
the only sign—and it was huge—
was lettered, simply, DOG LICENSES.
A routine mix-up, doubtless,

as this must be as well: "First
time for both?" The reply—a check
in the box provided, size of a thumbtack,
on a page with room for

marriages of the future—
applied equally to the best and worst
of intentions. As he supplied their proof
of blood, of residence, of birth,

she held her pen above
a line marked "Married Name": for who
she was, and what of She was He,
was not to be resolved

by closing time. Meanwhile, her
first footprint for signature,
no bigger than a cat's paw, he
paused to get the gist of. She

who on all his life to come
had laid a claim—staggering
in its singleness
of purpose—had once

been living, evidently,
only for minutes . . . Asked now to raise
right hands, to swear they knew
of no impediment,

he set down his tennis racket;
their eyes, for an instant long
to be remembered, gravely met
in the sweet embrace of fear.

EXPECTANCY

Japan Baptist Hospital, Kyoto

One by one, we shuffle in
and take a quiet seat beneath
admonitory posters. Here's
Mrs. Shimoda, who, to judge from
her pink, quilted jumper appliquéd
with rabbits, and a fuzzy, enormous purse
emblazoned with cartoon characters,

appears to be in some confusion
as to whether she's going to have a baby
or (a greater miracle) become one;
and here's sorrowful Mrs. Fukumoto,
who hasn't looked well in weeks. Of course
I'm guessing—I'm a newcomer here,
and as the nurse calls out each name

just a touch louder than necessary
in a kindly, patronizing singsong,
I flinch. Thermometer under tongue,
blood pressure measured, I can clearly see
a needle creeping on the hateful scale
where serene Mrs. Oh, five months along,
checks in at less than I at two.

Yet don't I, in fact, want to feel the weight
of waiting once again? the way
(years ago) each birthday took years to arrive . . .
Oh to be sixteen at last, to drive,
to come home past eleven! To loosen
the hold of parents who'd grown to fear
time as a thing they only got less of,
while you knew, yourself, it was stored within.

Too early, I know, I begin to imagine
how the baby turns in its own waiting room,
as restlessly as I now turn
a health-book page in a half-learned language:
Let's guard against (illegible);
be sure to (illegible) *every day!*

But here's the man who can read it all:
the doctor—handsome, young, a bit proud,
as if the father of all our children—
billows in on a white, open-coated sail
and, bowing to us with nautical
briskness, takes the time to wish
the mates a benevolent good morning.

We murmur in kind; then, in a hush,
some dozen heads in unison
swivel to follow his form until
it vanishes behind a door.
Daily, I think, women just like us
are found normal there. Who shall be the first?
It's Mrs. Hino—although the nurse

has to call her twice, across the length
of eight abstracted months. She rises
slowly, resting, in a universal
gesture I've only begun to read,
one hand on the swell below her breasts
as though what's borne within
were here, and could be taken in her arms.

JAPANESE CHARACTERS

I.

To look into a word as through a window
and address the thing itself: a simple wish,
and one calling me to a simpler time—
yet when can that have been? Life before English?
Conversant in the automatic doors
of an alphabet we barely need to press
for meaning sprung wide-open, now it seems
that again to sound things out and memorize
new, ramifying claims upon the eyes
is, piece by piece, to reconstruct a cosmos
I'd grown to think long set and spoken for.
Just as all life appears to have begun
the moment we were born, so around the sun
of native language orbit distant bodies
in atmospheres indigenously vague:
seen as through clouds, that's Venus thickly wrapped
in idioms colorful and yet inapt,
and Saturn's ring spins far too fast to wear.

The untold ideographs of Japanese
were Chinese first. To them are grafted two
syllabaries, native and phonetic,
which cling to borrowed roots. It grows aesthetic
to gaze upon these fruitless branchings, gnarled
so intricately no one in the world
can paint them right except a Japanese.
—Or so they'd have you think. Riding the bus,
my breath fogged on the pane, I puzzled out
streets whose billboards lettered in a scrawl
news that the world had slipped out of control.
Like insects some mad scientist had bred

to overrun an old, bad movie made
here in Japan, these characters were bound
to do us in . . . Enchanted, terrified,
at first I'd spend whole days cooped up behind
my room's milk-tinted glass. So little choice—
to view the brighter goings-on below
only by sliding free long streets of noise,
or to muffle them, but dim the light at once.

To look into a word as through a window
entirely clear—I'd given up that chance;
filmed over with the past, our TV screen
gave out on movies we'd already seen
at home. They'd been dubbed in Japanese,
but stubbornly, I felt as though I could
stare down the actors, coax them to unearth
my language lurking voiceless underneath.
Even at theaters, where we could hear
English so sharp we hung upon its edge,
characters white on black, and black on white
("subtitles" to the side, as hieroglyphic
as the crabbed marginalia on a page)
transported us to an unfeatured age
—past or future? it was hard to say—where night
is never clear enough to chart the stars.

II.
It's typhoon season. Above, a paper-thin
sky fills with figured clouds: an inky wash
the wind reconsiders swiftly with its brush.
Below, low-lying thunderheads (a queue

of black-haired students decked in navy blue,
each topped—like a dream of sun—with a yellow hat)
now and again burst out in laughter. Yet
they keep their civic files and parallels
that (paradoxically) might better suit
the strict march of our destined-to-repeat,
typecast, upstanding roman ABC's
whose measured zones our children (in their note-
books ruled like music staves) can fill
with nothing but the obsessive English trill.
How is it that the straitened Japanese,
living by Muzak and the megaphone,
tossed from such boats of reference stay afloat
with strokes on their letters fluent as a stream,
always familiar, never quite the same?
A mystery even when, some damp weeks later,
these start to take on clues of . . . character.

Each I could set apart from all the rest
began to stalk me—as, once, a night of cards
turned every dream to numerals for words,
and every one called out to be the last:
after I'd run through King and Jack and Queen,
thousands of faces beckoned me for names,
thousands of names for faces yet unseen.
Old women, bent at pained diagonals
like orchid grass; others in Western chairs
asquat on pliant feet, so that four legs
of wood then stood in place of two of theirs—
stamped on my brain as whole and legible
at last, they seemed to press a further claim
on life's behalf: *you're here to crack the code.*

In whiteface, wig, kimono, here's a Bride.
The Guests need not be guessed: identified
as men in black suits, ties of white brocade,
women in black kimono with a hem
brushed with bamboo or crane. They carry gifts
the right size for *furoshiki,* a square
of wrapping cloth that's often lavender.
Let there be no mistaking what we are,
they seem to say, *it's chaos otherwise;*
we'll limit human types to memorize.

III.

One day in the paper, there's a story
on an amateur astronomer—a factory
worker who, gazing on the stars
just before dawn with plain binoculars
("a part of my routine patrol," he said),
spotted a nova no one else had found.
"I know the sky quite well, but this was luck,"
he told reporters, "to catch it at its peak"—
three minutes of intensity before
a star we wake to think the only one
blotted with light all light except its own.

"I know the sky quite well"—a vivid claim
suggesting a nightly rummage through its shelves
of scorpions and saucepans. We ourselves
can't hope to re-arrange the stars, but name
and name again, as if to cut to size
chaos that takes us hugely by surprise.
Like stars, like snow . . . when clusters of words come,

some melt, a disappointment, on the tongue,
their mystery gone—and yet their calligraphic
descent to comprehension followed traffic
down streets untraceable on any map.
And in sculptured garden-ponds, I now expect
bridges of stepstones one line can't connect,
grammar reversing like a velvet nap
whose shade of meaning fades upon my touch . . .
Gravity's upended. The universe
observes, it seems, the old misspeller's curse:
You have to have things down to look them up.

What am I learning, then? Perhaps to wish
less fervently the Romans will march in
dispensing justice: for every man one vote,
for every voice a single character.
(What should we call the lanes between the stars,
or the silence burning even at the cores
of those so bright they make us feverish?)
Just as new words, once never seen, appear
on every page as soon as known, the sky
prints images upon the clouded eye:
distinguish these, and others will come clear.
Immersed in truths by half, the vertigo
of apprehending patterns through a window
rinsed clean—until it may well not be there—
one questions further. "What's next to the Bear?"

WELCOME TO HIROSHIMA

is what you first see, stepping off the train:
a billboard brought to you in living English
by Toshiba Electric. While a channel
silent in the TV of the brain

projects those flickering re-runs of a cloud
that brims its risen columnful like beer
and, spilling over, hangs its foamy head,
you feel a thirst for history: what year

it started to be safe to breathe the air,
and when to drink the blood and scum afloat
on the Ohta River. But no, the water's clear,
they pour it for your morning cup of tea

in one of the countless sunny coffee shops
whose plastic dioramas advertise
mutations of cuisine behind the glass:
a pancake sandwich; a pizza someone tops

with a maraschino cherry. Passing by
the Peace Park's floral hypocenter (where
how bravely, or with what mistaken cheer,
humanity erased its own erasure),

you enter the memorial museum
and through more glass are served, as on a dish
of blistered grass, three mannequins. Like gloves
a mother clips to coatsleeves, strings of flesh

hang from their fingertips; or as if tied
to recall a duty for us, *Reverence*
the dead whose mourners too shall soon be dead,
but all commemoration's swallowed up

in questions of bad taste, how re-created
horror mocks the grim original,
and thinking at last *They should have left it all*
you stop. This is the wristwatch of a child.

Jammed on the moment's impact, resolute
to communicate some message, although mute,
it gestures with its hands at eight-fifteen
and eight-fifteen and eight-fifteen again

while tables of statistics on the wall
update the news by calling on a roll
of tape, death gummed on death, and in the case
adjacent, an exhibit under glass

is glass itself: a shard the bomb slammed in
a woman's arm at eight-fifteen, but some
three decades on—as if to make it plain
hope's only as renewable as pain,

and as if all the unsung
debasements of the past may one day come
rising to the surface once again—
worked its filthy way out like a tongue.

HENRY PURCELL IN JAPAN

Here death does not confine itself
to the shuttered funeral parlor,
but roams from house to house like a beggar,
as quotidian as rain.
Today, once again, I saw them queuing
(the tail-coated men, black birds on a line,
the women columnar in kimono)
at a door where death had visited.
High bamboo placards draped in white
but muddied with sweeping characters
(names, perhaps, of those left behind)
were propped against the tiny house
like rafts secured to a bank.
Yet no one was going anywhere,

not the men whose task was to register
at felt-covered tables, brilliant red,
whatever was to be registered,
nor the women who made themselves at home
serving cups of pale green tea.
As I walked by they stared at me—
not angry, not stirring or saying a word,
but as if they expected me to concede
I didn't belong there. I remembered how,
standing in a Buddhist graveyard
some months ago—overseen by a crow
enormously foreign, and called *karasu*—
I'd known I was a trespasser.

It was their names that told me:
names recalled with unspeakable grace,

the chiseled letters liquid in stone
as if by brushwork. Reading down,
I felt as though the ashes of someone
whose name ran vertically might lie
differently, somehow, in the earth.
Such a small note seemed everything—
as today, once home from the funeral,
I listened to a choir sing Henry Purcell.
Rejoice in the Lord alway,
they sang; *And again I say rejoice!*
How explain to anyone the joy
of that single missing "s"—a winding path

down into a heritage so deep,
so long a part of me it seems
the very state of God?
The mellow, antiquated light
of drafty English chapels, and the comfort
of harmonies layered against the cold—
how exchange this god, like money,
for whatever imbues a Shinto shrine
painted the orange and gold of fire
with a bell-rung spirit more austere?
No, surely they were right,
the mourners who stared at me today;
schooled in other mysteries,
I stood as far from them

(or so it felt) as we all stood
from the foreign country of the dead.

Yet at home in my random corner
on truth, with no choice but to play
the world sung in a transposed key,
mine was another mourner's voice:
And again I say rejoice.

Unfinished Painting

(1989)

THE REBIRTH OF VENUS

He's knelt to fish her face up from the sidewalk
all morning, and at last some shoppers gather
to see it drawn—wide-eyed, and dry as chalk—
whole from the sea of dreams. It's she. None other

than the other one who's copied in the book
he copies from, that woman men divined
ages before a painter let them look
into the eyes their eyes had had in mind.

Love's called him too, today, though she has taught
him in her beauty to love best
the one who first had formed her from a thought.
One square of pavement, like a headstone (lest

anyone mistake where credit lies),
reads BOTTICELLI, but the long-closed dates
suggest, instead, a view of centuries
coming unbracketed, as if the gates

might swing wide to admit, here, in the sun,
one humble man into the pantheon
older and more exalted than her own.
  Slow gods of Art, late into afternoon

let there be light: a few of us drop the wish
into his glinting coinbox like a well,
remembering the forecast. Yet he won't rush
her finish, though it means she'll have no shell

to harbor in; it's clear enough the rain
will swamp her like a tide, and lion-hearted
he'll set off, black umbrella sprung again,
envisioning faces where the streets have parted.

READING ROOM

Williston Memorial Library,
Mount Holyoke College

The chapter ends. And when I look up
from a sunken pose in an easy chair
(half, or more than half, asleep?)
the height and heft of the room come back;
darkly, the pitched ceiling falls
forward like a book.
Even those mock-Tudor stripes
have come to seem like unread lines.
Oh, what I haven't read!

—and how the room, importunate
as a church, leans as if reading *me:*
the three high windows in the shape
of a bishop's cap, and twenty girls
jutting from the walls like gargoyles
or (more kindly) guardian angels
that peer over the shoulder, straight
into the heart. Wooden girls who exist
only above the waist—

whose wings fuse thickly into poles
behind them—they hold against their breasts,
alternately, books or scrolls
turned outward, as if they mean to ask:
Have you done your Rhetoric today?
Your passage of Scripture? Your Natural
Philosophy? In their arch, archaic
silence, one can't help but hear a
mandate from another era,

and all too easy to discount
for sounding quaint. Poor
Emily Dickinson, when she was here,
had to report on the progress of
her soul toward Christ. (She said: *No hope.*)
Just as well no one demands
to know *that* anymore . . . Yet
one attends, as to a lecture,
to this stern-faced architecture—

Duty is Truth, Truth Duty—as one
doesn't to the whitewashed, low
ceilings of our own. Despite
the air these angels have of being
knowing (which mainly comes by virtue
of there being less to know back then),
there's modesty in how they flank
the room like twenty figureheads;
they won't, or can't, reveal who leads

the ship you need to board. Beneath
lamps dangled from the angels' hands—
stars to steer us who knows where—
thousands of periodicals
unfurl their thin, long-winded sails;
back there, in the unlovely stacks,
the books sleep cramped as sailors.
So little time to learn what's worth
our time! No one to climb that stair

and stop there, on the balcony
walled like a pulpit or a king's
outlook in a fairy tale,
to set three tasks, to pledge rewards.
Even the angels, after all,
whose burning lamps invoke a quest
further into the future, drive
us back to assimilate the past
before we lose the words.

No, nobody in the pulpit
but for the built-in, oaken face
of a timepiece that—I check my watch—
still works. As roundly useful as
the four-armed ceiling fans that keep
even the air in circulation,
it plays by turns with hope and doubt;
hard not to read here, in the clock's
crossed hands, the paradox

of Time that is forever running out.

A CASE OF NETSUKE

Wise, size of a peachpit, nut-
brown, wizened, intricate,
　　the Badger Dressed in Lotus Leaf
stands tall in his sheet: as grand
or grander than Rodin's Balzac, and

even smacks of evil, as
he has the full, unruffled gaze
　　of the Wolf under Grandmother's nightgown.
The better to draw you close, my dear,
to a museum-case of obscure

Japanese bibelots. Each
a tangible anecdote, they reach
　　first to us from English tags:
Starving Dog, Herdboy with Flute,
Dutchman with Moneybag, or Stoat

on Pumpkin, Bean Pods, Pile of Fish . . .
As if that wordless, brimming wish
　　to get everything said before
we're dead might be fulfilled at last,
they speak to us of a lost

life we may have lived once, though
it's daunting we should think so—
　　for what could we have had in common
with Seated Demon or Drunken Sprite?
And by what twist does Thwarted Rat-

Catcher call up the aim of Art?
Yet that look of his, of being thwarted,
    as he crouches over the empty cage
and, too late, lifts his club to thwack
the rat scaling his own back,

is intimately familiar—like
the downturned, howling mask of tragic
    theater. If somehow the play
of his features also shows he's half-
laughing, it may be at himself:

grinning, with a shrunken skull's
grim triumph, or like a set of false
    teeth that's doubled over in
age-yellowed ivory,
he's detached from his unsavory

and blunt stabs at success. The gift,
he chides himself, is to be swift
    and tireless; to hit on a connection—
not just pummel the rat but tell
the whole tale in a nutshell.

THE MOON AND BIG BEN

STOP. Here, in our widened eyes,
they're nearly of a size.
And loom so close they seem to miss
    meeting by a nose,

the two moons of a pair of glasses
slowly disengaging as
the left one rises up to peer
    over the other's shoulder.

She finds there, in the Gothic news-
print of his measured face,
a daily mirror of the Times—
    the catalogue of crimes

and speeches, elections, electrocutions,
the columns and the revolutions
bringing new tyrannies to power
    almost by the hour—

and sees he stands for the imperial
notion of direction. The serial,
progressive sequence of events
    has, he booms, consequence.

Well. It is an ancient dial-
ectic, and it may take her awhile
(or forever) who whispers in his ear
    the limits of the linear

repeatedly, and every night,
to prove she has it right;
but there can be no gainsaying how,
    floating higher, smaller now

(and soon in ever-slimmer crescents),
she's not yet lost her essence.

UNFINISHED PAINTING

Dark son, whose face once shone like this,
oiled from well within the skin
of canvas, and whose liquid eyes
were brown as rootbeer underneath
   a crewcut's crown, just washed,

his body's gone unfinished now
more than thirty years—blank tent
of bathrobe like a choirboy's surplice
over the cassock's stroke of color,
   a red pajama collar.

Drawn as if it might reveal
the dotted hills of Rome, a drape
behind him opens on a wall
she'd painted with a roller once.
   Everything made at home—

she made the drapes, she made the boy,
and then, pure joy, remade him in
a pose to bear his mother's hope:
the deep, three-quarter gaze; the tome
   he fingers like a pope.

Is this the History of Art
he marks her place in, or—wait—
that illustrated Brothers Grimm
she'd inscribed for him, his name enclosed
   within it like a heart?

Hard to sort out . . . She rarely put
the final touch on anything
when he was young. It seems that bringing
the real boy up had taken time
   away from painting him

(no crime); she'd also failed to think
of him—back then her only child—
as truly done, and one child only,
but marvelled as he altered like
   the light she painted by.

. . . Like, too, the image he's retained
of the sun in her, now set,
her eyes that took him back, and in,
squinting as he squirmed, appraising,
   praising him again,

so that, when sifting through her basement
stacked with a dozen such false starts,
and lifting this one, lighter than
he thought it ought to be, to frame
   and hang in his apartment,

he saw in his flushed face how she'd
re-created there what rose
and fell in hers: the confidence
she forfeited each time she dared
   think of an audience.

Who (she must have asked) *would care?*
He does: that finished head conveys
still to him how, sought in a crowd,
a loved one stands apart—he's taller,
   comes in a different shade.

ELEGIES FOR ETSUKO

I.

Begin with the last and unrecorded scene—
how rashly, with a length of rope,
she'd gathered up an end to hope?
Or unravel these six years
to where my life first tangled up with hers?
Or, midway, to that greater knot: again

the line of thought loops back, heart-
broken, to where she reckoned life to start.
Her wedding day. The Bride.
And in truth, that day I shed
a veil of happy tears: to see that snow
mountain of kimono

and, falling from the pinnacle
of her lacquered wig, the fog of silk
over a face too shy, too proud
to lift. Who'd made her up?—the natural
milk of her skin absorbed in chalk,
a slope of powder

down to her collar, pulled low at the back.
Viewed from behind, a woman's neck
is (say the Japanese—and so she'd say)
her most erotic feature.
But I think she was that day
a hybrid sort of fantasy, a creature

sparked by a wand, then shrinking like that star
when the TV goes black. Am I unkind?
Darling, we guess at how you came unwound;
at how many times you drunkenly replayed
that trade of sacred *sake* and were made
Queen for a Day again on the VCR.

II.
Given how brief a spell
happiness usually is, and the ways
people are forever failing us,
with time it shocks me less you didn't mind
leaving the two of them behind;
yes yes, I see that, I see it very well . . .
But do you mean to say you were willing
never again to wear a new dress?
And never again to choose one for your daughter?
Long before she was born, or mine was,
we'd go on window-shopping sprees
in children's stores. Saccharine, but true.
I can't stand it, one of us would say; *can you?*
—A bonnet or a tasseled sock would send
us off: half-stifled, giggling cries . . .

In the end, you didn't think to find
even a rag to shield her eyes.
Because you had gone blind.

III.

In Keiko's brain these words are Japanese
in bits and pieces   none of them is written
nobody's here to hear the words she knows
nobody's here   just Mother on the ceiling
her face is closed her face   long face her hair
not crying now   she tries *okaasan*   Mother
the word that calls up everything
and nothing moves at all   oh there's her ball

IV.

Ages between the day I left Japan
and the first time I saw you again: the last
time, too. New Year's Eve in Rome.
Foreigners both, we soon pick up that word-
less, winking giddiness we'd had: as light
a burden as our daughters, whom we lift
to watch the soaring fireworks. Each time the sky
blows up again, and then begins to cry
in sputters—whistling, molten streaks of tears—
we laugh: *See? Nothing to be afraid of . . .*
And in the window, too, we see ourselves
reflected kindly in our girls: *They'll learn
to be mothers just like us.* How long since you
were known as Hara-san (Miss Hara)! These days
it haunts me, that when you married you erased
your first name too—and as an honor asked
I call you by a childhood nickname, Ekko.
Ekko. Echo. *Ecco:* the champagne

cork pops, the skies explode, repeat
that automatic gunfire to the heart:
Ekko, who would not toast the year again.

V.
These vacant months I've tried to disavow
that something's happened to you, something dire.
I know you're gone for good. And this is how

I've figured out you've made your final bow
(at last, the proof's so small that we require!)—
were you alive, you would have called by now.

More clues come than I'd willingly allow:
if they hadn't shoveled you into the fire
(I know you're gone for good, and this is how)

and buried you beneath a maple bough,
you would have dropped a line or sent a wire.
Were you alive, you would have called by now.

The phone's the lifeline of the lost *hausfrau*.
But now what's at your ear? The angel's lyre?
I know you're gone for good, and this is how

I turn the same line over like a plow,
since there is nothing further to inquire.
Were you alive, you would have called by now

to greet me in your faulty English grammar.
Your silence shows precisely how you are.
I know you're gone for good. And this is how:
were you alive, you would have called by now.

VI.

Up here's where you end up. Room with a view
in (of all places) Edinburgh, though who's
willing to predict she'll feel at home
with dying anywhere? Why not the random
furnished flat in Scotland? What we own,
what we are owned by, are no less transient
than other plots of earth we briefly rent . . .

Parking across the street, we stay inside
as if we hope (we fear) you're still up there
in a state of mind precarious but alive:
you mustn't be allowed to think we're spying.
You seem to know I knew I'd have to come;
that your husband's brought me here, a half-year later.
Oh, anything we do may set the chain

reaction going once more in that brown
study of your brain; we'd have to live
through losing you again; we'd have to choose . . .

Why is it your apartment's set ablaze
and no one else's? Why is it in the pitch
of six o'clock in winter, nothing's on
in all the building—just the silhouette

of a woman coming slowly to your window
to watch the Christmas lights down Princes Street
illuminate toy people and their things?
. . . Unless, somehow, you're giving us the ghost
of a chance to guess how singularly bright
you'd felt yourself to burn, engulfed in flame
none of us ever saw, much less put out?

VII.
Once, in Kyoto, we gossipped past the temple
graveyard where you'd lie, on to the shrine

where you wanted us to buy two paper dolls:
featureless, pure white, the kind a child

cuts in hand-holding chains across a fold.
An old priest had us sign them both for luck.

I wrote across the heart, you down the spine,
then quaintly (so I thought) you drew two smiles . . .

That was before you snapped your pretty neck.
Happy you may have been, but never simple.

VIII.

Happy you may have been . . .
There were whole years when I'd have said
you were happier than anyone.
You've now been dead

(and been enclosed
in the double mystery of what
that is, and why you thought
it might be best)

for long enough it's time
to more than forgive the sin
of express despair, the crime
of not being what we seem,

or of not being anything
in particular . . . for isn't that
really what you feared you were?
Sometimes the note

you didn't write (because
you needed all the energy you had
to do the deed? because
there's no cause in the mad,

for whom the world's a small
footstool kicked aside?)
looms real and legible.
It says you died

because you'd come to think that love
is not enough. Well, I'd
probably have agreed,
advised you to find work, to read.

And now love's pain, your curse,
is all I have. Forgive me . . . What worse
punishment for suicide
than having died?

IX.
On the master list we keep
imagining the scribes still keep
religiously, up there in space,
of every human life, let
them not neglect to fill the line
for Etsuko Akai, who's gone
    from Earth at twenty-eight.

In the impossible blue dark,
let all the bearded saints and rain-
bowed angels sorrow can invent
take her, who never made her mark,
and gladly mark the day for love
not of what she might have been,
    but what she humbly was.

For surely they have reams of time
to celebrate the perfect moon
set in her attentive face,
where pallidly, one shallow crater—
a pockmark time could not efface—
glossed the ancient and unwritten
    flaws of her Creator.

Since they will all be there for ages,
let them in their inventory
preserve in lucent, gilt-edged pages
those things I would myself record:
such as the way she'd tell a story—
she'd race, and trip, and laugh so hard
    we'd ask her to start over.

DOUBLES

Months later, when she's begun to breathe
more easily without him, she exhumes
    a roll of film, like a mummy, from
the camera's black chamber. Her memory
    of everything, not only him,

    has gone a little fuzzy—that's
a price she's had to pay—and in a rush
    she drops it off at the shop like sheets
she hasn't time to launder. It's all the same
    in the chemical bath, the surfacing frame

    after frame of grandchild, sunrise, garden—
and all the same to the man who hands them back
    to her, thick and bland as a deck
of never-shuffled cards. Yet when she deals
    them out on that snowbound night, she finds—

    somewhat to her surprise—the days
(each fenced in commemorative white border)
    again at her fingertips, and in order:
leafing from winter into fall, and fall
    into summer, a movie run in reverse,

    she's happy. And then she slows like a hearse.
It's him. Oh God, it's him. She thought she'd given
    all of him away—his ties
to the boys, his hundred handkerchiefs, his shoes—
    but here he is. There's more of him to lose.

Receive it like his posthumous postcard—a "wish
I were here"? How long did this message, curled as if
    in a bottle, wait to bring its proof
of some blue passage home from another world?
    Who took this last, lost picture? She can't

remember. Rooted here in her boots,
she knows it can't have been herself: she's *there*,
    in her tennis dress and fresh-permed hair;
she's living next to his seersucker shorts, the blinding
    glint on his glasses, the shine on his balding head,

she's standing with him behind the net
and squinting into an unseen sun—or, now,
    into the mirror of her own
face that has grown used to one alone.
    Dear man. If she could kiss that hand—

the hand he's flung across her shoulder,
warm from the game . . . But she understands no feat
    of athletic prowess will ever let
her jump that sagging net, and the game's unfair:
    the two of them against the one of her.

SUMMER 1983

None of us remembers these, the days
when passing strangers adored us at first sight,
just for living, or for strolling down the street;
praised all our given names; begged us to smile . . .
you, too, in a little while,
my darling, will have lost all this,
asked for a kiss will give one, and learn
how love dooms us to earn
love once we can speak of it.

AUBADE FOR BRAD

At six o'clock begins the ritual dance
of bumping into bureaus in the dark;
        it's time you went to work.
Holding one shoe at arm's length like a candle,
you grope for its mate, but stumbling on a sandal
        of mine, abandon hope
and ask for guidance in the softest voice;
I whisper too, as if there's still a chance
        we might not wake me up.

Once shod, you pull the creaking blinds whose slats
narrow their sleepy eyelids into slits,
        and I'm to take the cue
more sloth is my reward for finding you
the means by which you'll disappear till dinner.
        Condemned to write
from dawn until you drop in bed at night,
you'll spend a happy, virtuous day convinced
        you are a miserable sinner.

No doubt it is the hard fate of the Writer
to suffer like the rest, but not know better
        than to call it a job. What's worse
than feeling so deeply one must doubly force
oneself to show it in both prose and verse?
        I sympathize, of course;
so much, in fact, I'd joyfully disprove
that formula by which all Energy
        converts to (Printed) Matter

and devote, this morning, some of it to Love.
    Darling, if you'll untie
    your shoes again and lie
for a moment here, while the sun turns all to gold,
    I may grow very bold.

DEAD LETTERS

I.

Dear Mrs. Salter: Congratulations! You
(no need to read on—yet I always do)
may have won the sweepstakes, if you'll send . . .
Is this how it must end?
Or will it ever end? The bills, all paid,
come monthly anyway, to cheer the dead.
BALANCE: decimal point and double o's
like pennies no one placed upon your eyes.
I never saw you dead—you simply vanished,
your body gone to Science, as you wished:
I was the one to send you there, by phone,
on that stunned morning answering the blunt
young nurse who called, wanting to "clear the room."
"Take her," I said, "I won't be coming in"—
couldn't bear to see your cherished face with more
death in it than was there five days before.
But now, where are you really? From the mail
today, it seems, you might almost be well:
Dear Patient: It's been three years since your eyes
were checked . . . A host of worthy causes vies
for your attention: endangered wildlife funds,
orphans with empty bowls in outstretched hands,
political prisoners, Congressmen. The *LAST*
*ISSUE*s of magazines are never last.
And now you've shored up on some realtors' list,
since word went out you've "moved" to my address:
Dear New Apartment Owner: If you rent . . .
Mother, in daydreams sometimes I am sent
to follow you, my own forwarding text
Dear Mrs. Salter's Daughter: You are next.

II.
When I try to concentrate
on who you were,
images of you blur
and pulsate, like the clothes
left in your closet—

every size from four to fourteen,
not progressively,
but back and forth again:
testaments to Treatment
after Treatment.

Injected, radiated,
bloated, balded, nauseated;
years in an iron wig that ill
fit or befitted you;
then more years, unexpected,

of a cobweb gray you grew
in thanks to covet:
lurching from reprieve to reprieve,
you taught yourself to live
with less and less,

and so did we—
even, at last, without the giddy
vastness of your love,
so painfully withdrawn when pain
became all you could think of.

Trying not to feel
that nothing, not even love
or death, is original,
like other mourners I've
turned up happy photographs—

of the ruby-lipsticked girl
(in black-and-white, but I can tell)
on your wedding day; or, here, a scene
in a hallway I'd hardly know was ours
but for that gilt barometer.

Had I lost that about you?
Your regal touch—china in green
and gold; silk Oriental dresses?
. . . Days that made you queen
of nothing but your high-backed bed

convinced you
you'd been singled out to die.
Yet here you are,
a smiling hostess at the door
bidding your friends goodbye:

What blessedness!
—To think that once
you hadn't had to be the focus,
could go on living unpitied,
even unnoticed.

III.
Dinner in Boston. I am twenty-three,
and you have come to see
your grown-up daughter in her element.
My choice is cheap and almost elegant:
crêpes and spinach salad, a carafe
of chilled house wine we laugh

companionably over. Memory drifts
back to well-set tables shared at home—
those animated dinners you would chair
(the Salter Seminars, my boyfriend called them)
where you taught me to admire
the complex givens of your gifts

for life. Accomplished cook,
stickler for decorum, you liked to shock
us with the heedless, vocal sweep
of your opinions: on the Catholic Church
(you hate it, so you think—hate it so much
you'll find a slow way back);

the saintliness of Adlai; Armageddon.
(Once, you greeted me from school with news
the Chinese had invaded us: a thrill
that never found its way to print,
but you shrugged off my complaint:
"If they haven't done it yet, you know they will.")

Tonight, Newbury Street—
scene of my happy lunch hours, of the young
executives with ice cream cones

dripping down their hands, bright students in new jeans—
outside our window takes, as night sifts down,
that memorializing cast of light

you seem to shed on things, all by yourself.
Even when all is well (the illness
more under control than less,
you're devoting all your time to sculpture
bigger than you are—filling every shelf
in the garage!) I still recapture

moments before they're over.
She loved me so, that when I praised her shirt
she took it off her back, or
We drank four cups of tea apiece . . . Alert
always to what perishes, I invert
your low, confiding chuckle now and pour

its darkness like a stain across our table.
"Can you remember Grandma's laugh? I can't,"
I interrupt, and having voiced the fear,
immediately am able:
it sounded like a baby's xylophone,
thrown down a flight of stairs.

Who could have forgotten *that*?
I laugh myself—but now I've spoiled
the mood, or turned it oversweet,
and you reach into your magic purse
for a snapshot of your mother. "Here, it's yours."
Stunned how soon my eyes have filled

with tears—how easy it has been
to give a pleasing answer—
you seem relieved to put to death
a momentary fright not only mine.
Now, your own forever-
unrecorded voice cut short by cancer,

I still find myself asking: dear
as she was, didn't you know
it's you I was crying for?

IV.
We're on our way to the hospital
for the twenty-thousandth time.
You used to drive—then I;
lately, we've piled into a taxi.
Each week a new man takes the rap
for bumps and jolts; if not for him
(you imply) we'd have a pleasant trip.
Shrunken and old, collapsible,
head in my lap, you start up in alarm:
"Mary Jo—I think I'm ill."

Forgive me that I laughed!
It's too late to apologize;
but that you could find it in you still
to register surprise—
that *you'd* hope to be well . . .
It kept you alive, of course,
those years of asking visitors

"Are your ears ringing?" as if there might
someday be found a blanket cause
for pains that kept you up all night.

V.

If you could see your daughter, no green thumb,
tending the philodendron
you sent me when my baby girl was born!
If you could see my daughter: that refrain
twists like a crimping weed, a vine of pain
around the joy of everything she learns.

And yet it intertwines
forever, I perceive, your life and mine.
From time to time, a heart-shaped leaf will turn
yellow and fall—in falling a leaf torn
out of your life again,
the story I must constantly revive.

I water it and live;
water and wait for other plants to bloom.
I took them from your room
nearly a year ago now, poinsettias
of that wizened, stricken Christmas
you floated through five days before the end.

One's inky-red; the other paper-white . . .
You too were one to note
life's artful correspondences.
But I can't let them go,

not yet; and granted time to tend
a growing tenderness, I send

more letters, Mother—these despite
the answers you can't write.

Sunday Skaters

(1994)

WHAT DO WOMEN WANT?

"Look! It's a wedding!" At the ice cream shop's
pristine picture window, the fortyish
blonde in the nice-mother shorts and top
stops short to raise two cones, one in each hand,
as if to toast the frothy blur of bride
emerging from St. Brigid's across the green.
"Mom," a boy answers, "I said I want a *dish*."
But this washes under her, while a well-matched band
of aqua-clad attendants pours outside
to laugh among fresh, buttonholed young men.

Young men . . . remember *them*? Her entourage
now is six boys, and she buys each one his wish.
When she peers up from her purse, the newlyweds
have sped away, and she notices at last,
on the littered steps of the Universalist
Society, some ten yards from St. Brigid's,
a rat-haired old woman in a camouflage
Army-Navy outfit, in whose pockets bulge
rags, or papers, and an unbagged beverage.
Looks like a flask of vodka. But no, it's dish-

washing liquid! It's Ivory, the household god.
The shape is clear from here: a voodoo doll,
headless, with the waist pinched, like a bride.
Poor thing—her dirty secret nothing worse
than the dream of meals to wash up after. While
what *she* most craves, standing at this font

of hope, the soda-fountain, with the boys
all eating hand-to-mouth, is not to miss
the thing that . . . well, it's hard to say; but what
she'd want, if we were given what we want.

BOULEVARD DU MONTPARNASSE

Once, in a doorway in Paris, I saw
the most beautiful couple in the world.
They were each the single most beautiful thing in the world.
She would have been sixteen, perhaps; he twenty.
Their skin was the same shade of black: like a shiny Steinway.
And they stood there like the four-legged instrument
of a passion so grand one could barely imagine them
ever working, or eating, or reading a magazine.
Even they could hardly believe it.
Her hands gripped his belt loops, as they found each other's eyes,
because beauty like this must be held onto,
could easily run away on the power
of his long, lean thighs; or the tiny feet of her laughter.
I thought: now I will write a poem,
set in a doorway on the Boulevard du Montparnasse,
in which the brutishness of time
rates only a mention; I will say simply
that if either one should ever love another,
a greater beauty shall not be the cause.

YOUNG GIRL PEELING APPLES
(Nicolaes Maes)

It's all
an elaborate pun:
the red peel of ribbon
twisted tightly about the bun
at the crown of her apple-

round head;
the ribbon coming loose in the real
apple-peel she allows to dangle
from her lifted hand; the table
on which a basket of red

apples
waits to be turned into more
white-fleshed apples in a water-
filled pail on the floor;
her apron that fills and falls

empty,
a lapful of apples piling on
like the apron itself, the napkin,
the hems of her skirts—each a skin
layered over her heart, just as he

who has
painted her at her knife
paints the brush that puts life
in her, apple of his eye: if
there's anything on earth but this

        unbroken
    concentration, this spiral
of making while unmaking while
    the world goes round, neither the girl
        nor he has yet looked up, or spoken.

INSIDE THE MIDGET

In town again some ten years later,
led by new companions to
a flashy restaurant—Chinese—
I know it like I know my face.
Whatever it was . . . why can't I think?
Sitting before a blank

placemat, as at an exam—or worse,
the dreams of exams one had back then,
of never having taken the course—
I hear my ears pound when a friend
whispers the impossible answer:
"This used to be the Midget Deli."

The Midget! It was half this size.
I thought everything was supposed to shrink
when one came back. They must have torn
down the wall between the rooms; then
refurnished, refinished, refined until
there's nothing left we'd recognize—

Darling, you should be here. How many
Sunday mornings did we stumble in,
hung over, egging the other on
to order feasts we'd barely touch?
("Some toast, at least. Soaks up the wine.")
Where's our exhausted, pickle-faced waitress

who'd extract a pad and pencil from
the marsupial pouch in her uniform?
Thick-rimmed as a bathtub, white
but ringed with a tannin stain, the mug

of tea she'd bring had the bag already
soaking in lukewarm, shallow water,

limp tag like a dangling arm.
One can grow nostalgic over anything,
it seems. Tonight, the tea pours hot
from a metal pot into porcelain.
Much better—which is hard to admit
to that happy pessimist, still dressed

in jeans and college black, whose heart
(she tells me) beats beneath my pearls.
Ten years ago? No—twelve, thirteen.
And think of it: grown-up even then,
as, over some table here (no X
to mark the spot) your eyes would meet

mine in one thrilling thought—*Last night*—
and nothing need be said.
Look: I'm shaking. I can hardly find
the ladies' room without a guide,
and then the lady in the mirror
isn't the one I was seeking out—

she looks more like my mother. I know
that tender, disappointed frown;
she gave it to some midget
version of myself (two front teeth
missing) who'd just ripped a skirt.
But *now* what have I done

to feel so guilty for? Was I
the one who chose to gut the place?
Or to gild the walls, as if space fills
equally well with true or false?
The door swings open: in the dining room
I can see at once the counter where,

above a pastry-case of strudel,
a plastic dome like a crystal ball
housed yesterday's last bagel.
They're opening fortune cookies there,
chuckling at strips of paper far
too small, from here, to read.

JUNE: THE GIANICOLO

Driven to this, the pairs of lovers roll
into the parking lot like shaken dice,
and though they've come expressly for a vista
much grander than themselves, begin to fuse
into the other's eyes. Oh, that fond conviction
of a match made in Heaven!
                           Below them, at the base
of an ancient hill, the million lamps of Rome
light up in rosy approbation, each
signalling to one chosen counterpart
among the stars the nightly freshened wish
to lie uniquely in its dazzled gaze.

THE TWELFTH YEAR

That autumn we walked and walked around the lake
as if around a clock whose hands swept time
and again back to the hour we'd started from,
that high noon in midsummer years before
when I in white had marched straight to my place
beside you and was married and your face
held in it all the hours I hoped to live.
Now, as we talked in circles, grim, accusing,
we watched the green trees turning too and losing
one by one every leaf, those bleeding hearts.
And when they all had fallen, to be trod
and crumbled underfoot, when flaming red
had dulled again to dun, to ash, to air,
when we had seen the other's hurts perfected
and magnified like barren boughs reflected
upside-down in water, then the clouds
massed overhead and muffled us in snow,
answered the rippling lake and stopped the O
of its nightmare scream. The pantomime
went on all winter, nights without a word
or thoughts to fit one, days when all we heard
was the ticking crunch of snowboots on the track
around the lake, the clock we thought we either
were winding up or running down or neither.
Spring came unexpected. We thought the cold
might last forever, or that despite the thaw
nothing would grow again from us; foresaw
no butter-yellow buds, no birds, no path
outward into a seasoned innocence.
When the circle broke at last it wasn't silence

or speech that helped us, neither faith nor will
nor anything that people do at all;
love made us green for no sure cause on earth
and grew, like our children, from a miracle.

POPPIES

I.

For years, above the white sofa, it hung
as a shimmering emblem of home—
the path white-hot, the blurred
strokes of the loaded brush Renoir meant
to convey summer's plenty and the rush
of the child who led the way.
They were going home

through a heedless field of green and yellow,
weeds tickling ankles, insects ticking—
a mass of happiness.
Just steps behind the child was a woman,
the pulsing heart of things, the red
parasol behind her head
a medal of motherhood, a halo,

and here and there, the red parasols
of poppies were twirling on their stems,
each held safely by the hand
of roots unseen in the soil.
There was so much you couldn't see.
No house beyond the gate on the right.
No face on the two black-clad

figures descending from the crest
of the hill. Grandparents, I decided.
That dot was her big black parasol.
No telling how long an inch

of canvas might take them, or if they'd catch
up ever. But the child had lost,
as it gained on them, nothing as yet.

2.

Staring into the postcard,
I follow the shrunken path
upward until the black
parasol, with a surreal
insouciance, leads me back

behind the hill, far back
to a television screen
where I saw this only once.
I would have been six or seven,
now old enough that a cold

meant no school, and I lay
in my parents' bed like a queen.
Mother was out in the garden,
my lunch was on the tray,
and a movie in black and white

flickered with nuances
I was happy not to get.
Then a door slammed. And the mother
in a long, old-fashioned dress
was rushing out the gate,

a mammoth black umbrella
above her averted face.
Thunder was splitting things,
and the violins explained
that this was really the end,

and the child cried at the window
filmed from the outside
so you couldn't hear the tears
running down with the rain.
I was locked in bed, and the movie

was taking the mother away,
and frame after frame was a door
shutting fast, and I had no key.
When the child knelt to peer
through a keyhole in the shape

of a teardrop, I understood
she was never coming home.
How long could the little scene
of abandonment have taken?
I turned it into a dream,

and played it over and over
until it became one seamless
parable that arched
from parasol to umbrella,
a place to search for cover

before I woke and found
the nightmare dried
to nothingness in the sun.
You—you've now been gone
ten years; been dead longer

than I'd lived when I learned
you'd leave forever.
Ten years ago, beneath
the shelter of some tree
or other, as you'd asked,

your child stood with an urn
of ashes, and scattered them
to the breeze, as if a random
handful might crop up
in the field as poppies.

LULLABY FOR A DAUGHTER

Someday, when the sands of time
invert, may you find perfect rest
as a newborn nurses from
the hourglass of your breast.

LAMENT

Waking in her crib, the boat
they pushed her off in long ago,
although she stood to shake the rail
and wail at them,
                she's all at sea.
Nothing familiar in the dark
until she rubs it from her eyes:
gray bear, gray ceiling where the moons
and stars turn, turn away.
                    Why
wouldn't she cry? For out there, perched
at table's edge, unreachable,
white to the brim, supremely real,
the bottle with the golden nipple
glows like a lighthouse.

THE AGE OF REASON

"When can we have *cake*?" she wants to know.
And patiently we explain: when dinner's finished.
Someone wants seconds; and wouldn't she like to try,
while she's waiting, a healthful lettuce leaf?
        The birthday girl can't hide her grief—

worse, everybody laughs. That makes her sink
two rabbity, gapped teeth, acquired this year,
into a quivering lip, which puts an end
to tears but not the tedium she'll take
        in life before she's given cake:

"When I turned seven, now," her grandpa says,
"the priest told me I'd reached the age of reason.
That means you're old enough to tell what's right
from wrong. Make decisions on your own."
        Her big eyes brighten. "So you mean

I can decide to open presents first?"
Laughter again (she joins it) as the reward
of devil's food is brought in on a tray.
"You know why we were taught that?" asks my father.
        "No." I light a candle, then another

in a chain. "—So we wouldn't burn in Hell."
A balloon pops in the other room; distracted,
she innocently misses talk of nuns'
severities I never knew at seven.
        By then, we were Unitarian

and marched off weekly, dutifully, to hear
nothing in particular. "Ready!"
I call, and we huddle close to sing
something akin, you'd have to say, to prayer.
     Good God, her hair—

one beribboned pigtail has swung low
as she leans to trade the year in for a wish;
before she blows it out, the camera's flash
captures a mother's hand, all hope, no blame,
     saving her from the flame.

ICELANDIC ALMANAC

1. *The Sky in Akureyri*
in July is high and broad,
with here and there a scrap of cloud
stretched like a hat that doesn't fit.

Nothing can put a cap on it,
this light that lasts all night,
even when the long, elliptic sun,

a low plane circling for an open
runway, nearly lands—
but, throwing up its hands, ascends

by slow degrees again.
After a while, though every motion
tends to the horizontal, what

you're hoping for isn't sundown but
rainfall: something to precipitate
the end of a relentless,

restless Paradise.
Time an eternity of space . . .
Time watching as dark, overblown

clouds hold their breath all day, then
drily fly away; time beaten thin
enough it may have passed

entirely into mist.
When at last the first
cloud dissolves, like a tablet

in its own water, it's also like a thought,
whose moving parts are discrete, caught
in the murky downpour of feeling.

But this is not the end. Trailing
behind with its blanket, failing
to see what can't be done, the sun

resumes that setting—or sitting—on
a fine, pink line it's drawn
to divide today from tomorrow.

II. *The Dark in Reykjavik*
        in December is far
        from monolithic—not
a block of static blackness, but
        an inky, effervescent

        potion ever
    carbonated by the dots
of thousands of electric lights.
    The stars are burning

ceaselessly somewhere, and here
you remember that: orderly
stacks of them, floor by floor.
And neon at eleven in

the morning makes
everything you've done so far
(breakfast, getting dressed) appear
precocious, blazoned triumph—

trumpeted, as well, by twin
high beams turning corners for
the dark at the end of their tunnels; or
by inverted funnels thrown

from a line of streetlamps.
Not monolithic, no, and yet
come noon when, like the spangled velvet
drape the poet speaks of, night

parts (a space enough
to poke your face through; a spotlit
hour or two a playwright might
illuminate the limits of

our life in), gratitude
rises up. Even for that wall-to-wall
cloud rolled across the sky, as dull
and sullen as a pearl,

whose muffled glow
    forecasts another sort: not sun-
shine's diamond, and meant more to be seen
    than see by; obscurity

    dressed in white;
    sub-zero understudy flown in from
everywhere at once—in sum,
    snow filling in for light.

SUNDAY SKATERS

These days,
the sky composes promises
and rips them to pieces. White
as a sheet, this morning's cloud-
cover crumples now and again, then snaps
back white when a gust shakes it out. Out
for the usual stroll,

I stop
to look at March in its muddles:
in a snowbank (black
boulders of old ice new-
mottled with powder), puddles
that must be from yesterday's
slanting rain and hail,

which fell
as if from one combined
salt-and-pepper shaker. I wind
as the wind does, chased downhill,
past the soaked, concrete blocks
of apartments and the dented heaps
of corrugated-iron houses

left out
in the rain for years and years,
the olive-green of their raised
surfaces sprayed with rust
in vertical bands. Venetian blinds—
more metal, pulled to metal sills, but
going against the grain—

      mix up
the texture, as does, still better, this
     one lace-curtained window fringed
      with icicles.
    Since they may melt in an hour,
on a day when everything's changed
    so often, one pauses for that pristine

      tension
of winter held in suspension. Just
     then, at the bottom of the street,
      I see the skaters:
    the luck of it
on a Sunday! The chances thin
    as the ice they coast on—

      to find
the snow wind-dusted off,
     and an hour both cold and warm enough
      overlapping leisure.
    From here, the disc of the pond
looks like one of those children's games
    designed for the palm,

      whose goal
is all at once to sink each silver
     ball into a hole.
      What each of them is slipping
    into, though, is another color:
approached, they glide by in mint and mauve
    and lilac, turquoise, rose, down

parkas
in shiny nylon glimpsed
for an instant. Like a clock
with too many hands, gone haywire,
the pond's a rink of hockey sticks: tock-
tick-tick as the puck
takes a shortcut from four to six

to nine.
Look at that girl in the long braid, trailed
by her mother, a close-cropped beauty
who takes on a heart-speeding
force, as they spin hand-in-
hand, and a teenager's sheen;
and catch that baby buggy,

pushed off
freely as a swing down the ice . . .
Stock still at the clock's center,
the pin that everything hinges on:
the wide, fur-circled face
of a small boy who feels his place
in the larger frame.

It's all
about time, about time! Above us,
a frosty layer of cloud takes the weight
of the sun's one warming foot,
bright as a yellow boot. Although,
as yet, nothing flies but the snow's
negative (flurries

                of crows
appearing from nowhere), rather
        than wait for the other shoe
                to drop—that shower
        of rain, or sleet, or something, sure
to come—I rush into a coffee shop,
        and close the door.

        And close
my eyes, in time, when a cup
        of muddy, quivering liquid releases
                erasing clouds of steam, calling up
        in the sudden dark the skaters' dizzy
scissoring and see-sawing, scoring
        lines over, and over again.

THE HAND OF THOMAS JEFFERSON

1. *Philadelphia, 1776*
War had begun. And one could hear its drums
in the psalm of scorn he ranted at the tyrant.
"He has refused . . . He has forbidden . . . He
has plundered our seas . . .": so the verses went
from the hand of Jefferson, at thirty-three
the youngest of the committee whose assignment
was to authorize a nation. In rented rooms

on Market Street, he borrowed arguments;
dependent, in the cause of independence,
on the common sense of Paine and the untamed
logic of Locke, the reason wrenched from treason,
his passion was original, but he claimed
invention of no more than the design
of the portable desk his words were resting on.

What rested on his words, though, he could guess.
Adams and Franklin let the rough draft pass
with scarcely a revision. Now the debate
struck out much more: his outcry at the "market
where MEN should be bought & sold." Foiled, he learned
firsthand, at least, a government by consent.
He bowed to the majority, and was governed.

That morning—it was the fourth of July—he'd bought
a thermometer. Praised after by the Great
Emancipator for his "coolness" and "forecast"
in seeing through an end to monarchy,
the man of science literally passed

its final hours in silence and the neat
recording of a rise in the mercury.

The apex came at one in the afternoon:
seventy-six, the aptest of temperatures.
Jefferson must have held up to the light
his instrument, and read it like a vein
pulsing with the newborn body's powers.
"The earth belongs to the living," he would write—
out of his hands, henceforward into ours.

2. *Paris, 1786*
        After a decade of marriage, his
        dear Martha, following hard on the birth
of their sixth child, belonged to the earth
        at Monticello. "Unchequered
        happiness" will be his phrase
        for their time together; whether or not,
as legend has it, she begged him from her deathbed
        never to marry again, the record
        has it he never did.

        For days, weeks, the knife of grief
        pinned him to his room; he paced
as if movement alone proved him still alive;
        then, hour upon hour, he rode
        on horseback with his daughter Patsy past
        the checkered plot of gravestones under
which more children lay, to the forest
        where no calling could reach his hearing. Or
        so he believed at first.

But a bayonet
can become a baton; sometimes we're given
a wound that won't allow us to refuse
to carry on. Now it was Congress
that gave him a cause: mission
abroad. For the Minister to France,
four years wifeless in the summer
of '86, a blooming readiness
for romance feels like a rumor

he needs someone else to start.
Paris, grander than anything,
is expanding; on longer and longer walks
from the Hôtel de Langeac, he ducks
under scaffolding and falls
in love with whatever's going up.
A hammer in the architect's heart
pounds when a manned balloon clears a tree,
rising from the Tuileries.

The circle of his acquaintance
is growing too, and when his artist
friend John Trumbull brings some guests
along to the Halle aux Bleds, the grain
market whose slatted wooden dome,
like an upended sifter, lets the sun
drift inward, the widower all at once
is enlightened by the giddy sense
that the woman standing next to him

may be his, as he is hers.
Maria Cosway is her name:
a painter and musician, Italian-
born, a resident of London—
not here for long. Yet who among us is?
She has a husband, but he's small;
a painter too, he excels at miniatures.
How easy to dismiss him as
they enlarge the boundaries

of Paris: over their heads
that August night, a firework display
makes molten blueprints of more domes
that boom and vanish in the sky.
Explosions followed by long day
excursions: Saint-Germain-en-Laye,
le Château de Marly, le Désert de Retz . . .
In September, though, it's in the heart
of town they end their games:

hopping a fence, head over heels
for her, he trips and falls. The wrist
of the hand that wrote the Declaration
has snapped, the right one, never to be set
properly again. And the pain
is compounded when—no liberty
to prevent it—she's ferried home to London:
Cosway's property, Jefferson's happiness.
Feeling, as the wheels

of his carriage, or ill fortune, speed
him away from their farewell, "more dead
than alive," somehow he's strong
    enough by October to write another
    remarkable text in his career:
    four thousand words of love
in his left hand. A dialogue of "my Head
    and my Heart," he calls it, a debate of left
    with right, more than right with wrong,

    and if Heads win, it's by an edge
    thin as the rim of a coin. Must
we lose everything we love? Well then,
    let us have it first, at least,
    and take a political consolation:
    "if our country . . . had been governed by
its heads instead of its hearts, where
    should we have been now?
    hanging on a gallows

    as high as Haman's."
    The broken-hearted optimist
seals the envelope with his broken wrist,
    and closes a chapter in his life.
    For though Maria returns
    for a season to Paris, though she writes
letters in broken English that burst
    into Italian, as if into tears,
    though they correspond for many years,

September of '86 has fractured
their time into before and after. Another
revolution is soon to happen:
    friends on all sides will lose their heads.
        He who can wave away the shots
        of Shays' Rebellion ("the tree
of liberty must be refreshed from time
    to time with the blood of patriots
        and tyrants") can't foresee

    the flooding of his beloved France.
    And secure, for now, in the belief
its uproar will be rational and brief,
    in '89 he plans, calm after the storming
        of the Bastille, to settle
    some business affairs in America.
"I count certainly to be here" in Paris
    by May, he writes Maria; that "charming
        month" must close their distance—

    but the city in chaos, and greater forces
    than her marriage, or the rippling arm
of La Manche (held up so long between them
    like a policeman's) conspire to make
        that passage across the Atlantic
    his last. Spring of '90 finds her changed.
Trying to find his tone, in phrases
    fusing affection and something foreign,
        he writes from Monticello, "They tell me

que vous allez faire un enfant."
    —A daughter whom she'll abandon, to run
not to Jefferson but the continent;
        though she crawls home to Cosway,
            nursing their child, and him, to the end,
        her own last years are spent at the convent
school she founds in Italy. One wall,
        she plans, should depict the "academical
            village" her friend has built in Virginia.

        He'd posed, soon after Maria left
        Paris in '86, for Trumbull,
who'd introduced them. Omniscient men at a table
        have signed a Declaration. The crippled hand
            of its author healed, the handsome
        face a decade younger, his heart made whole
once more, Martha's eternal husband,
        he is painted into the simpler role
            posterity will assign him.

3. *Monticello, 1826*
Long ago, when he was President,
        he'd open up the White House door
to the public on two weighty days a year,
        each with two meanings. Reticent

at any cost about his private life,
        he chose the first of January
to note general renewal. (Who knew but he
        when Martha had become his wife?)

Second, the fourth of July—the nation's date
    of Independence that fell
just at mid-year (a mathematical
    boon he was born to appreciate)

held within itself, more secretive
    than he, another message so
cryptic his own Creator alone can know.
    We never guess it while we live.

Nor could John Adams, old firebrand and friend
    and enemy, have suspected on
New Year's 1812, when he'd put pen
    to paper, and their estrangement to an end,

they'd end in tandem, nearly to the hour.
    For over a dozen years now, they've
had time to lament their slide toward the grave;
    having learned to share their power

uneasily once, as skeptical Federalist
    and blithe Republican, the Sages
of Quincy and Monticello scrawl long pages
    on their competing frailties. The wrist

is stiffer, Jefferson writes, and Adams shakes
    illegibly with such a palsy, he
(half-blind as well) regards his friend with envy—
    a friend who, nearing eighty, breaks

his other arm in a fall . . . This time he trips
        on the terrace his right hand had traced
into existence, a little rise he'd placed
        to step up to the mountaintop's

one shifting, never-finished house. The left
        wrist cracks, and when the fingers swell
importantly, the fatal flaw they spell
        this time is mortality itself—

the fall of a common man, whose ancient horse,
        named for the national bird, could soar,
poor Eagle, hardly higher any more
        than he. And yet one could do worse

than gamely hand the reins to one's successors.
        Even before Adams passed
the Presidency to him, with a last
        protest of appointments, a source

of their contention lay in how much hope
        one dared place in the future. "The generation,"
Jefferson sees, "which commences a revolution
        can rarely compleat it." Whether Europe

will ever complete it is the question hanging
        over the two old rebels. A fickle heart
has seen France through her flings with Bonaparte,
        and now, as Adams notes, she changes "king

as easily as her glove." At home, the fate
        of the Union haunts him more than when
all his fears were heaped on Independence.
        Faithful that "a future State"

awaits us, and that he and the Virginian
        will meet there soon enough with all
their loved ones—for he's lost his Abigail—
        he has a more divisive vision

of a government on earth, in which the "black
        cloud" of slavery that passed
into their time, and—somehow—hasn't burst,
        won't be persuaded to turn back:

it's packed with soldiers. "Armies of Negroes marching . . .
        in the air" are coming. But he can't
command "the genius of Franklin, to invent
        a rod" that might extract the lightning.

Nor can Jefferson, whose love of science
        is less a bolt from the blue than the steady
husbandry of data. Once he seemed ready
        to free the slaves in a flash; but his sense

of impotence has deepened, along with debt,
        and unable to compute a way
to free his own, he has no more to say.
        Unable to conceive a blanket

emancipation, nor a society
     where black and white are knit as one,
he wraps himself in a "mantle of resignation"
     and wishes, above all, to be free

forever of the subject. His time is over.
     He'll take the answer to his grave
whether he fathered children with his slave,
     Sally Hemings; what words he'll offer

to cover himself are buried in a drawer,
     meant for his tombstone. Here lie three
accomplishments (he skips the Presidency):
     the Declaration; the Virginia Statute for

Religious Freedom; and the University
     of Virginia. Though he discounted
this last to Adams—joking he was "mounted
     on a Hobby"—the truth has made him fly

back forty years to France, and an afternoon
     he rode with Maria to Marly, where
a water "Machine" threw rainbows in the air,
     and the king's pavilions drew a line

he would copy for the campus in Charlottesville.
     His own past and the world's combine
by design; he's even brought the Pantheon
     of Rome to the new Rotunda. For all

of an hour, not long ago, he'd watched men haul
    Italian marble for its bases
and columns from the Rivanna River. The places
    he'd hoped to shape!—like the Capitol

in Washington. He'd wished, then, that its dome,
    like a mind raised up from swamp, could call
for inspiration on the airy Halle
    aux Bleds, in which she'd turned to him

in a blaze of light . . . They say it's razed by fire.
    They say the nation's Rotunda fills—
he trembles like Adams—with the light of Trumbull's
    paintings of revolution, and more

copies made for the cause. He'd have the men
    who come to his university
understand this: originality
    is knowing what to copy, and when.

And why to amend: it could be that the mantle
    of resignation he puts on
is reversible in the flick of a wrist, a gown
    of commencement, of graduates who will tell

the story right and wrong, but not by
    memory alone. And then it will be theirs,
their revolution. He hears now on the stairs
    the footsteps of his daughter Patsy,

his sole child left, his mainstay. She's come to take
　　his temperature, perhaps—then
he slips into unconsciousness, and when
　　he struggles, one more time, to wake,

he asks again: "Is it the Fourth?" Of course
　　it is, they lie (it's still the third),
and though he dies with barely another word,
　　he waits until the clock-hands cross

midnight, and past noon. Jeff Randolph holds
　　his grandfather's wrist up, and it pulls
his heartstrings when the vein resigns its pulse;
　　he shuts the eyes, and slowly folds

one swollen hand across the other. The Fourth
　　of July is fifty; Jefferson's eighty-three.
The South Pole of the Revolution, as he
　　is known already, faces North

to Massachusetts where John Adams lives
　　a few hours more in ignorance
and wisdom so that, dying, he'll pronounce,
　　"Thomas Jefferson survives."

If, as Adams wrote to Jefferson,
　　a "boyish Firework" is all the universe
can add up to, should no life follow ours,
　　that night the fireworks whistle for his son

who occupies the White House. Though too feeble
    to attend the galas, in advance
Adams had given Quincy "Independence
    Forever!" as a toast, and the fable

grows monumental when the speech that goes
    to the capital from Jefferson—
"All eyes are . . . opening to the rights of man"—
    is read the day his own eyes close.

Once called a demagogue, now demigod,
    he rises hand-in-hand (one eulogist
among the many shrouding him in mist
    will say) with his long-distant friend

to Heaven; in Boston, Daniel Webster roots
    for words in a three-hour oration;
but the future guards its secrets from a nation
    that looks up at the flaming rockets

in the sky for augury. Another war
    is drumming up, but not before the shrine
of Monticello tumbles into ruin,
    Patsy penniless, the hammer

that built her house now traded for the gavel
    of the auctioneer who splits
whole families her father owned to bits,
    unfreed by law or his good will,

and the country's shifting house still barely stands
    undivided. But had he watched the exploding
fireworks, he might have seen unfolding
    millions of brilliant hands.

FROM

A Kiss in Space

(1999)

FIRE-BREATHING DRAGON

    Impossible, and yet I seem
  to be dropped in the basket like a cut
flower trembling on its stem;
    am arranged with the others by a pilot
who keeps firing from a tank of gas
    an ear-blasting dragon's mouth of heat
unbearable to look at; and straight
    as an elevator the *montgolfière*

    lifts in unfettered calm. Silence
  now, and limitless; no glass
between us and the world we clear
    of nailed-down roofs and trees that appear
in the breeze to be tethered balloons.
    A boy bursts out of his house—runs
and runs as hard as he can to the edge
    of the yard and can't endure the hedge

    that stops him; if he'd only run
  faster, his outstretched arms are saying,
he'd have taken off like a plane.
    Everybody's waving. All
our feelings grow keener and simpler: *Bonsoir!*
    Bon appétit! Bonsoir! we call
fervently to our nameless friends
    sitting down to a *plein air* supper.

    —As if none of them had ever toiled
  to till a field; as if these rows
of wheat had never been combed by plows;
    as if the tangled necklaces
of white-blossomed *petits pois* in their flung-

open jewelry box of soil
were conundrums we can leave unraveled;
   as if what really matters

     is *our* happiness above all, we sail
   on their wave of blessing over the sun
itself which, although hugely afire
   on the scarlet horizon, hasn't blown
up in going down. A whoosh
   of flame from time to time supplies
to our buoyancy an unneeded push;
   already it's impossible

     we'd ever assent to landing, or
   follow any command but those
of the puffed-up, roaring heart.
   Look!—far in the distance—that double
puncture in the making is Chartres.
   A worthy foil, or choice of foils,
to spar with, that singular pair
   of spires: mismatched because a fire

     eight centuries ago had taken
   an early steeple down. Even
from here, the miniature blaze
   of stone that rose up in its place
is a towering flamboyance,
   and from our own we think we peer
not only far but back—to time's
   processional of nameless pilgrims

struggling below us on that very
   path until the wheat fields parted
like gates to reveal the painted portals
   of Heaven on Earth, the saints
not yet wind-stripped of color, and winged
   Pride in fresh relief forever
falling from his horse. Once,
   people believed in dragons—

   as we began to, an hour ago,
      drifting to such a height the tinted,
interlocking shapes of crops
      became a story in stained glass
our shadow could fall into. Now,
   as if cabled to the sun that drops
off the rim of the world, we start
   to descend; the snap of treetops

   snagging under our basket turns
      the stomach a little; the pilot turns
to me gallantly with a leaf bouquet
      snatched in midair and suddenly
we're kissing (as he says) the tall
   grasses hissing under us,
before we buck like a bronco to
   a halt that is not a fall.

   Still, who wouldn't feel deflated
      to see our St. George kill the dragon?
Wrestling to the ground its noble
      yard on yard of whistling nylon,
he pounds it like a punching bag

into a flattening triangle
to fold repeatedly like a flag
    at a military funeral.

    Giddy, as one is when all
    is lost (who can deny a May
evening so visionary comes
    just once if ever?), we laugh and fill
the blanks in ready-made diplomas
    with the vanity of our names;
we fill our glasses with champagne
    whose balloons by the hundreds rise.

WRECKAGE

Torn from the moorings of sleep
one morning, grasping not even a scrap
of whatever I was dreaming,

I realize, as I rise from the billowing
sail of the pillow, and sink again,
that I myself am wreckage

from the ship that smashed miraculously
the instant it broke
consciousness; am driftwood

toyed with at the edge of the tide,
a floating, disembodied arm
left to record the dream

it does not remember, while all the other
passengers heavily go down
to an oblivion where no

plumb line of a memory
of having had a memory
can reach. I alone on the beach

am real, and stand at last to fill
the funnel of the coffee filter
with spooned black heaps of sand,

watch as the hourglass spills the grains
of millions of associations
drop by drop in the O

of sentience that swells to a runnel,
smells like thought and is drinkable
and clarifies the thinking:

so early it's already too late
to say I never wanted to cross
into a wholly rational state,

to upend the coffee grounds like a sand
castle into the sink and rise
to the occasion of day, another

impermanent construction washed
down the drain; didn't want to dissolve
in the shower now these unseen cells

in the foam—little parts of the selves
I can't be part of anymore;
didn't want to walk away dry.

A RAINBOW OVER THE SEINE

Noiseless at first, a spray
of mist in the face, a nose-
gay of moisture never
    destined to be a downpour.

Until the sodden cloud
banks suddenly empty
into the Seine with a loud
    clap, then a falling ovation

for the undrenchable
sun—which goes on shining
our shoes while they're filling
    like open boats and the sails

of our newspaper hats
are flagging, and seeing
that nobody thought to bring
    an umbrella, puts

up a rainbow instead.
A rainbow over the Seine,
perfectly wrought as a draw-
    bridge dreamed by a child

in crayon, and by the law
of dreams the connection
once made can only be lost;
    not being children

we stand above the grate
of the Métro we're not
taking, thunder underfoot, and
soak up what we know:

the triumph of this *arc-
en-ciel,* the dazzle
of this monumental
prism cut by drizzle, is

that it vanishes.

A LEAK SOMEWHERE

No toy in a bathtub, the Titanic;
but on our twenty-one-inch screen
it's faintly laughable, as Barbara Stanwyck
and her daughter in their lifeboat gasp
at the sight of the great vessel sliding
into the North Atlantic like a spoon.

Yet only faintly laughable.
When the ship blows up, with Stanwyck's son
and husband on it, the four of us
(warm beneath one blanket flung
across a comfy sofa in
the lifeboat of our living room)

bob with the waves of melodrama.
How ironic! Their family had split
even onboard, but along other lines:
living abroad had spoiled the girl
(Annette was so pretentious she
addressed her fellow Yanks in French),

but Norman, with his normal name,
might still be saved in Michigan.
Or that was Stanwyck's plan. And now
he's sinking with shallow Clifton Webb,
his Paris-besotted father, to
a depth where such distinctions are all

for naught. The ship's a symbol of
society, we tell our children—
belowdecks, into the porthole maws
of furnaces, bare-torsoed men

stoke coal until their sweat runs black;
when the iceberg slices through the hull,

they're flooded in an instant. Above
in steerage, the crammed-in families
of the kerchiefed, overexcitable poor
race for the door and, as water climbs,
scramble upstairs where Guggenheims
and Astors (so well-bred they barely

raise an eyebrow even for
historic personal disasters)
set down their hands of bridge, and don
life jackets like the latest fashion.
Not enough lifeboats? Noblesse oblige,
everybody at once is noble,

and an instinctive revolution
reshuffles the classes: women and children
first. Down the Jacob's ladder
of rope they struggle to the shaky
safety of going on living, while
those left behind on the heavenly

height of the tilting ship take solace
in their perfectly rehearsed rendition
of "Nearer, My God, to Thee."
Oh, you and I can laugh. But having
turned off the set, and led the kids
upstairs into dry beds, we sense

that hidden in the house a fine
crack—nothing spectacular,
only a leak somewhere—is slowly
widening to claim each of us
in random order, and we start to rock
in one another's arms.

VIDEO BLUES

My husband has a crush on Myrna Loy,
and likes to rent her movies, for a treat.
It makes some evenings harder to enjoy.

The list of actresses who might employ
him as their slave is too long to repeat.
(My husband has a crush on Myrna Loy,

Carole Lombard, Paulette Goddard, coy
Jean Arthur with that voice as dry as wheat . . .)
It makes some evenings harder to enjoy.

Does he confess all this just to annoy
a loyal spouse? I know I can't compete.
My husband has a crush on Myrna Loy.

And can't a woman have her dreamboats? Boy,
I wouldn't say my life is incomplete,
but some evening I could certainly enjoy

two hours with Cary Grant as *my* own toy.
I guess, though, we were destined not to meet.
My husband has a crush on Myrna Loy,
which makes some evenings harder to enjoy.

LIBRETTO

Libretto. That's the first Italian word
    she wants to teach me: "little book."
This afternoon (but why are we alone?
    Were Daddy and my brothers gone
all day, or has memory with its flair
    for simple compositions air-
brushed them from the shot?) she's set aside
    just for the two of us, and a lesson.

On an ivory silk couch that doesn't fit
    the life she's given in Detroit,
we gaze across the living room at the tall
    "European" drapes she's sewn
herself: a work of secret weights and tiers,
    hung after cursing at her own
mother's machine. She lets the needle fall
    onto the record's edge; then turns

to pull a hidden cord, and the curtain rises
    on Puccini's strings and our front view
of shut two-car garages, built for new
    marriages constructed since the war.
Well, not so new. It's 1962
    and though I'm only eight, I know
that with two cars, people can separate.
    He went away; came back for more

operatic scenes heard through the wall
    as if through a foreign language. Muffled
fury and accusation, percussive sobs:
    they aren't happy. Who couldn't tell
without the words? *Libretto.* On my knees

the English text, the Italian on hers,
and a thrill so loud the coffee table throbs.
    I'm following her finger as

we're looping to a phrase already sung
    or reading four lines at a time
of people interrupting and just plain
    not listening, and yet the burden
of the words is simple: Butterfly must die.
    Pinkerton will betray her, though the theme
rippling above him like a hoisted flag
    is The Star-Spangled Banner. Mother, why

would a Japanese and an American
    sing Italian at each other?
Why would he get married and not stay?
    And have a child he'd leave to wait
with the mother by the screen with her telescope
    for the ship of hope? Why, if he knew
it wouldn't last, did he come back to Japan?
    —But I'm not asking her. *That's men*

is her tacit, bitter answer; was always half
    her lesson plan. *O say, can you see . . .*
yes, now I can. Your dagger's at the throat
    and yet I feel no rage; as tears
stream down our faces onto facing pages
    fluttering like wings, I see you meant
like Butterfly to tie a blindfold over
    a loved child's eyes: the saving veil of Art.

For it is only a story. When the curtain
    drops, our pity modulates
to relief she isn't us, and what's in store
    for you, divorce and lonely death,
remains distant. We have our nights to come
    of operas to dress up for,
our silly jokes, our shopping, days at home
    when nothing is very wrong and in my chair

I read some tragedy in comfort, even
    a half-shamed joy. You gave me that—
my poor, dear parents, younger then than I
    am now; with a stagestruck, helpless wish
that it wouldn't hurt and that it would, you made
    me press my ear against the wall
for stories that kept me near and far,
    and because the hurt was beautiful

even to try to write them; to find that living
    by stories is itself a life.
Forgive whatever artifice lies
    in my turning you into characters
in my own libretto—one sorry hand
    hovering above the quicksand
of a turntable in a house in Detroit
    I can't go back to otherwise.

DISTANCE

From up here, the insomniac
river turning in its bed
looks like a line somebody painted
so many years ago it's hard
to believe it was ever liquid; a motorboat
winks in the sun and leaves a wake
that seals itself in an instant, like the crack
in a hardly broken heart.

And the little straight-faced houses
that with dignity bear the twin
burdens of being unique and all alike,
and the leaf-crammed valley like the plate
of days that kept on coming and I ate
though laced with poison: I can look
over them, from this distance, with an ache
instead of a blinding pain.

Sometimes, off my guard, I half-
remember what it was to be
half-mad: whole seasons gone; the fear
a stranger in the street might ask
the time; how feigning normality
became my single, bungled task.
What made me right again? I wouldn't dare
to guess; was I let off

for good behavior? Praise
to whatever grace or power preserves
the living for living . . . Yet I see the square
down there, unmarked, where I would pace

endlessly, and as the river swerves
  around it, wonder what portion of
love I'd relinquish to ensure
    I'd never again risk drowning.

ALTERNATING CURRENTS

1. *Reading in the Dark*
   Imagine, if you will, a hotel
room fronting Niagara Falls. Helen
Keller has been brought here by
her teacher, Annie Sullivan,
to meet their good friend Dr. Bell,
inventor of the telephone,
who has long worked with the deaf.
Helen, thirteen, already known
around the world for having thirsted
at the well of knowledge in her own
backyard, where Sullivan had spilled
water in one hand and spelled
the word into the other, now
lets him lift her hand in his
like a receiver, and gently press
it flat against the window's ear.

   The glass is cold. And through her splay
fingers a liquid thunderbolt
of vibration charges and discharges
at once, so thrilling in its force
that she nearly tastes the spray—
though, one must add, the girl is made
of words more than of anything
by now; she feels what she's been told.

   Teacher gave her half the world
she knows. How to fathom, then,
the ingratitude that surfaces
in dreams? At Radcliffe, later, where

Teacher sits through every class
and unabsorbedly (for she's
a medium, a conductor, and what
greater sacrifice?) transmits
directly to her charge's hand
all the professors' lectures, she
appears sometimes in Helen's nightmares
as a quarrelsome tormentor,
driving her to "an abyss, a perilous
mountain pass or rushing torrent."
Once "I saw her robed in white
on the brink of Niagara Falls."
Her costume seemed to be an angel's.
When she dropped into the whirlpool,
Helen, frantic, dove in to pull
Teacher from danger; the figure wrestled
out of her arms and swam to shore
untwinned. And this—the unthinkable
thoughtlessness of one who loved her—
was the purest terror.

But how lucky she is! Instead of toys
they bring her famous men: William
James, W. E. B. Du Bois,
Oliver Wendell Holmes, Mark Twain.
One day she'll touch Caruso's voice.
Somebody in Gardiner, Maine
has named a lumber vessel for her.
Hers is a fate that launched a ship.
At her fingertips, the Braille
armies of words amass: she scans

The Iliad in the original.
(What is original? She hasn't
dared to ask since, at eleven,
a story she had thought she thought
up wholly by herself had proven
to be the tale of a "plagiarist.")
Sometimes she is just as glad
not to tire Teacher, and will work
late into the night—but then,
she writes to kindly Mrs. Hutton,
"one wearies of the clash of spears
and the din of battle." No one hears
the punctured pages turning as
she soldiers on alone, the blind
reading the blind: the lovely Helen
following Homer in the dark.

2. *The Final Problem*
    Across the ocean, an oculist,
Dr. Arthur Conan Doyle,
plots the ultimate crime. He boasts
to his mother, "I think of slaying Holmes . . .
& winding him up for good and all.
He takes my mind from better things."
Twirling the weapon in his hand,
he pens the title: "The Final Problem."

    Deflecting blame, perhaps, he sets
the end on foreign soil. A train
of reasoning takes Holmes and Watson

to Switzerland, fleeing that regal
rival, the "Napoleon
of crime," the spider in a vile
network of radiating evil.
(Too bad. Had Conan Doyle more art, he
would have created Moriarty
long before.) Face to face
at last, detective and nemesis—
their twin defiance heightened by
the pointed altitude of the Alps—
peer at each other in a bliss
of imminence. The great men tumble
in a wrestler's grip together
down the Reichenbach Fall—unseen
by Watson, who runs up too late.
Yes, that's very good. He'll call
helplessly down the abyss
to hear nothing but his staggered voice
crack open on the cliffs in echo.

    Yet, blinded by the cataract
of his invention, Conan Doyle
can't see the problem isn't final.
Holmes can no more (the public's logic
runs) have perished in those falls
than Falstaff had on the battlefield.
Or had at rough words of Prince Hal's.
Like Shakespeare, who obeyed the queen's
command to resurrect his rascal,
in time the doctor bows to pressure,
dries off his hero, sends him home—

and calls the stories *His Last Bow.*
It's not, of course. Some characters
wake forever in the middle
of their lives: the rooms in Baker Street
are perpetually fixed in place
like letters Holmes speared with a jack-
knife to the mantelpiece; his fiddle
case is never closed.

    Left unsolved: how a B-plus
stylist, Conan Doyle, who preferred
what he called "psychic research," and,
touchingly gullible, obtuse,
finished up his own career
believing in fairies, should have had
the cool to track down the great sleuth
within himself, the cynical
logician who could see in the dark.
Liar, master of disguise,
Holmes elegantly cloaks the thin
transition of two eras: loyal
subject of The Exalted Person
(unnamable Victoria), he's
already prone to modern ills.
Ennui is The Final Problem—for which
there's but a seven percent solution,
or target-practicing indoors
(poor Mrs. Hudson!); with the flair
of one in deep despair, he marks
the whole wall in a manly Braille:
"V.R. done in bullet-pocks."

How in the world could Conan Doyle
come up with an unkillable myth?
"When you have eliminated all
which is impossible," as Holmes
repeatedly explains, "whatever
remains, however improbable,
must be the truth."

3. *Hearing Shadows*
    President Garfield has been shot,
and Alexander Graham Bell
hops on the train for Washington
to find the bullet. It's lodged somewhere
in the body of the President,
and though he's not a medical man,
Bell hopes to provide a tool.
His "induction balance," as
he calls it, like his "photophone,"
is work that follows in a line
from the telephone—which made his name
six years ago. Disengaged
sometimes from himself, he wonders
if he really *had* invented it.
Or was it someone he'd read about?
That's not a doubt to speak aloud,
with everybody and his brother
daring to claim the patent. "The more
fame a man gets for an invention,"
he once confided to the page,

"the more does he become a target
for the world to shoot at."

   The photophone has given him
a synesthetic thrill he's known
only in poetry. (And though
he's far too busy to notice how
he phrases things, that letter to
his father last year was poetry.
"I have been able to hear a shadow,
and even have perceived by ear
the passage of a cloud across
the sun . . .") Insert selenium
in the telephone battery; then throw
light upon it, thus altering
resistance, and varying the strength
of the current sent to the telephone.
An image, then, may have its own
correspondent sound. Simple.

   "Watson, come here, I want to see you":
that's all that people can retain,
tending, as people will, to miss
the point. It wasn't just Tom Watson
on the other end of the line,
it was the Telephone in Real
Form he'd wired at last to an
Ideal one floating in his brain.
The question is if he can do
the same again: the deadly ball
sits humming somewhere silently
for his machine to answer it.

He's swept into the White House by
a private entrance. How to enter
the President's body without harm?
He scans the skin with his instrument,
hoping to trigger an alarm.
Three days later, the victim drained
of a once florid cheer, the bullet
like a whole note sings a clear
tone for one measure. Bell returns
to his lab in Massachusetts, fiddles
in vain, more misery intervenes:
his baby boy is born and dies.
Then Garfield does. The autopsy
reveals the bullet had always lain
too deep for a safe extraction—
which hadn't, in fact, been necessary.
A death caused mostly by infection:
doctors' unwashed hands.

In the history books, poor Garfield
is footnoted for being killed.
But Bell goes on to re-invent
himself, a man who—as he'd said
when the telephone was still afloat—
is lost in fog, and yet can tell
his latitude and longitude.
He takes notes on condensing fresh
water from real fog; conducts
genetic trials on sheep (but fails
to name any of them Dolly); constructs

one flying machine—less like a plane
than a giant paper honeycomb—
after another. "I have not
the shadow of a doubt," he writes
in 1893, "the problem
of aerial navigation will
be solved within ten years." The Wrights
will get there first. But in his way,
as always, he's right on the money.

4. *A Tangled Skein*
   " 'From a drop of water,' " Watson reads
aloud from a magazine, " 'a logician
could infer the possibility
of an Atlantic or a Niagara
without having seen or heard of one
or the other.' " He slaps this down
on the table. "What ineffable twaddle!"

   It's his first wrong move. The essay's
author, we've foreseen, is Holmes,
his brand-new roommate, about whom
this "Study in Scarlet" proves the first
in scores of chronicles that he—
that is, Dr. Watson—writes.
Dr. Conan Doyle's rough draft
called it "A Tangled Skein." And we
might too, this craft of authorship.

So let them, on my tangling lines,
call the overloaded switchboard
for souls they're linked to, all at once:
Keller and Sullivan, Conan Doyle
and Watson, Bell and Watson, the two
two-watt Watsons, Sullivan
and Watson (either one will do:
all three are listening to this list
and taking notes), Holmes and Watson,
Holmes and his flip side, Moriarty
(not yet heads-first over the falls),
and since the distinction's always fine
between detection and invention,
Holmes and Bell, then Holmes and Bell
(a Dr. Joseph Bell) whom Conan
Doyle had partly modeled Holmes on.

    What are they saying? Something about
"the scarlet thread of murder" that runs
"through the colourless skein of life."
That's Holmes—who, in his arrogance
(but no one else can do it right),
kills himself a little with
more cocaine in his scarlet vein.
Something more about resentment
of whatever we have cause to call
ourselves. And yet we'd ask for foils,
for second fiddles, for noble, dim
Watsons as constant witnesses.
Holmes to Watson: "It may be that

you are not yourself luminous . . .
but you are a conductor of light."
Bell to Watson: "Come here, I want
to see you." Holmes to Watson again:
"Come at once if convenient;
if not convenient, come all the same."
And this: "Come, Watson, the game's afoot!"

    And what's the game? Something about
taking a message. A scarlet thread
of reception branches in the brain,
a filament, brilliantly unclear
except for clearly being there—
like the lightbulb waiting to switch on
in the head of half-deaf Edison—
and Conan Doyle is not entirely
wrong, as he joins the conversation,
to add: "I felt that my literary
energies should not be directed
too much into one channel . . ."

    Bell bellows into the phone: "Hurrah!"
(Nobody can ever convince him
to settle for a simple "Hello.")
"Hoy! Hoy!" These days, an older man
embodying an anagram
(as a boy A. Graham Bell had gone
by the alias of "H. A. Largelamb"—
destined, it seems, to experiment
on sheep), he doesn't use the phone
very often anymore. The ring

annoys him at the dinner table;
besides, his wife—the winningly
named Mabel, the original
Ma Bell—is deaf. She writes to us
instead, an essay on the art
of lip-reading. A misnomer. The kiss
of unheard word with thought must come,
she says, by marking body clues
(eyebrows, hands); on the lexicon
of context; and, since very little
is ever understood at once,
on empty-headed readiness
to miss a detail. You can feel
your way back to the blanks.

    Which is the decoding task of Holmes.
The scarlet "Rache" the victim scrawls
on the wall is quickly misconstrued—
if you only read one language—
as "Rachel." But it means revenge.
One letter. What he seeks may hinge
on anything. The dancing men,
a child's line of stick figures, turn
murderous with a hypothesis—
the commonest figure must be "E"—
and Holmes unlocks the cryptogram
so well he tricks the criminal
to present himself for arrest in his
own dancing language: "Come at once."
The flesh made word, the word made flesh.

Half-blind Annie Sullivan,
nineteen, untaught, is summoned to
Tuscumbia, Alabama to tame
a child who doesn't know the name
of anything. Then she has a thought.
"I had no idea a short while ago,"
she writes a friend, "how to go to work;
I was feeling about in the dark;
but somehow I know now, and I know
that I know." She's going to pretend,
for now, that Helen understands.
Keep talking. From a drop of water,
a single word, a Niagara
untangles in their hands.

MR. X

By the time you're forty, you've met so many people
their features fall in place as little bits
from other people, like the Identi-Kits
that victims piece together with the police.
The felon is memory, which takes a face
and slices up what once was very simple.

People you loved, the waiter you saw every week
without seeing, arresting strangers re-assemble
years later in other faces and belong
convincingly there, as if they were unique,
and innocent of how they make you tremble
with remembering or forgetting. I was wrong,

Mr. X—whose cheekbones I recall
from somewhere, and that funny, slightly cross-
eyed, quizzical look you shot me on the sole
occasion we met—to assume you must have lost
someone who looked like me. And yet I stared
longingly at you, as you disappeared.

THE SEVEN WEEPERS

The tines of his comb were splitting into finer
brittle strands, like hair, but his own hair—
deader than a corpse's, which can lengthen
in the sweet cool of the coffin—had stopped growing.
Screws unscrewed themselves from wooden boxes
where the stone-dry food was kept. Matches ignited
magically in air, as they fell to earth.
And who would believe it? When he took his pen
to paper, to record the temperature—
a hundred fifty-seven in the sun,
in the shade a hundred thirty-two—the ink
dried at the nib; the lead dropped whole from pencils.
What he had wanted was to draw a line
on the map from Adelaide into the heart
of the outback, where he'd willed a vast Australian
sea like the Caspian. But water holes
of a single shrinking creek were all they'd found,
like the globules of a burst thermometer.

Worst, he thought, was how the rising moon
offered no respite—so blinding that the black
swans that flew across its surface seemed
charred in the passage. Mostly, nothing moved
but ants and lizards. He who had fought
with Wellington against the French, who'd quelled
riots in Ireland, and headed a convict guard
all the way to the wrong end of the world,
where summer raged in January, now
had loitered with his men and bulls and horses
by a nameless pool, with debilitating wisdom,
six months for a drop of rain. In July it came.

And watered them enough to drag themselves
safely for a while across the blank
he named the Stony Desert, with a compass
that couldn't tell them when they should turn back
from infernal sandhills, burnished red, so hard
the horses left no track, as in a dream.
Twice they retrenched and shifted course when hope
of water dried up, shallow and absurd:
a pigeon diving steeply into shadow
that might be mud but wasn't; a clump of bush.
In November a seagull, five hundred miles from sea,
led them to a salt lake, purplish blue,
the color of Heaven.

                    What then was this scene
of misery they'd stumbled on? Years later
in England, nearly blind, Charles Sturt would wake
some mornings to that sight of seven naked
black men in a circle by the lake,
wailing and weeping. So profligate! he thought,
spending their grief like that. Who knew
when it would rain again, or if the sun
would bake away this pond of indigo
to nothing? Fools. Better save your tears.

Some in his group knew tribal words, and tried them.
What was the matter? A death? But all the words
were wrong, and the seven weepers seemed
as if they'd long forgotten what it meant
to have an answer. Inconsolable
is all they were.—Somewhere beyond the terror

he'd caused once, early on, in native eyes,
when he'd come bounding forward on his horse.
It wasn't the horse, exactly, but himself
dismounting from it: apparently they'd thought
white man and horse were one, a sort of Centaur.

And yet there were no Centaurs, no such creatures
ever in their heads: the thought now struck him
with the beating of the sun (or so the tale
would go if one retold it as one chose,
too far from 1845 to say
what any of them were) that these were men
wholly unlike himself. What songs they chanted
into the air could only evaporate,
though their chimeras—like the man-sized snake
and the red, preposterous kangaroo—were real.
Hath the rain a father? Or who hath begotten
the drops of dew? That voice, which thundered now
in the groping cloud of dust that was his mind—
where had it come from?—was of course the voice
of God in the whirlwind, chastising his servant.
And hadn't Job lost seven sons? What help
that fact was to him, he could hardly say,
but he stood there wrapped in silence while the naked
sinners wept, until he could remember
that Job had sat for seven days in silence
before he spoke.

                  He didn't have a week
to wait for them; his handkerchief was a rag.
Charles Sturt, whose nation soon would drape its flag

over the weepers' country like a shroud,
reached from his Christian soul and in the heat
uselessly, kindly, gave them his overcoat.

ABSOLUTE SEPTEMBER

How hard it is to take September
straight—not as a harbinger
of something harder.

Merely like suds in the air, cool scent
scrubbed clean of meaning—or innocent
of the cold thing coldly meant.

How hard the heart tugs at the end
of summer, and longs to haul it in
when it flies out of hand

at the prompting of the first mild breeze.
It leaves us by degrees
only, but for one who sees

summer as an absolute,
Pure State of Light and Heat, the height
to which one cannot raise a doubt,

as soon as one leaf's off the tree
no day following can fall free
of the drift of melancholy.

AU PAIR

The first thing she'd noticed, as they sat her down for lunch
by the picture window, was flags all doing a dance
in front of houses: was today a holiday?
No, they said smiling, it's just the American way,
and she couldn't help reflecting that in France
nobody needed reminding they were French,

but the neighborhood had turned out very nice,
no fences, big yards, kids racing back and forth;
you could let the shower run while you were soaping
or get ice from a giant refrigerator's face.
She couldn't believe how much the franc was worth
and she had no boyfriend yet, but she was hoping,

and because her father was the world's best baker
she naturally thought of his bakery in the Alps
whenever they passed her a slice of their so-called bread,
and sometimes she wished she could hire a jet to take her
back just for breakfast, but as her great-aunt had said
so wisely more than once, it never helps

to make comparisons, so she mostly refrained.
She couldn't believe, though, how here whenever it rained
the mother sent children out without their coats,
not carelessly, but because she had no power
and nobody made them finish the food on their plates
and bedtime was always bedtime plus an hour,

so au pairs were useless really, except for the driving.
Yes, that was puzzling: after she cracked up the car
they didn't blame her or ask her to pay a thing,
but once she let Caitlin eat some sort of cherry
with red dye in it, and then they *were* angry, very.
Americans were strange, that much was clear:

no penmanship, and lesbians held hands
on the street, and most women carried a pair
of pumps in a bag they never took out to wear;
it was so disrespectful, she couldn't understand
how older ones got called nothing, not even Madame,
but then nobody in this country had a last name

which was going to make it hard to write them a letter
when she got back. It was really bittersweet
her visa was running out; she was sad that all
she'd done with her days off was go to the mall,
she'd bought a million T-shirts and that was great
but she had to admit it, saving would have been better,

and she knew somehow that when she got on the plane
she'd probably never live anywhere foreign again
which filled her American family with more pity
than she felt for herself, because at least she was coping,
she'd work at her sister's shop and stay in the city
where she had no boyfriend yet.   But she was hoping.

LIAM

He's down again, aswim in a dream
of milk, and Teresa who is far
too tired to go back to sleep goes back
to the table where she tests the nib
of her pen, like the nipple on a bottle.

Into a bottle of permanent ink
she dips her pen and begins to trace
over her pencil-marks on the face
of the spiral scrapbook the name they chose
for him who has never dreamed of a name.

It's *William*, like his father, but
she has only got as far as *Will*
(the doubled *l* another spiral
to the *Liam* they now call him), which
leaves her still three letters to spell

the man who's curled up in *I am*.
—The stranger in the crib who seems
longer each time they lift him out
and will find that while they named the story
it is his to write.

A KISS IN SPACE

That the picture
in *The Times* is a blur
is itself an accuracy. Where
this has happened is so remote
that clarity would misrepresent
not only distance but our feeling
about distance: just as
the first listeners at the telephone
were somehow reassured to hear
static that interfered with hearing
(funny word, *static,* that conveys
the atom's restlessness), we're
not even now—at the far end
of the century—entirely ready
to look to satellites for mere

resolution. When the *Mir*
invited the first American
astronaut to swim in the pool
of knowledge with Russians, he floated
exactly as he would have in space
stations of our own: no lane
to stay in, no line to determine
the deep end, Norman Thagard
hovered on the ceiling something
like an angel in a painting
(but done without the hard
outlines of Botticelli; more
like a seraph's sonogram),
and turned to Yelena Kondakova
as his cheek received her kiss.

And in this
   too the blur made sense: a kiss
   so grave but gravity-free, untouched
by Eros but nevertheless
   out of the usual orbit, must
make a heart shift focus. The very
   grounding in culture (they gave him bread
and salt, as Grandmother would a guest
   at her dacha; and hung the Stars
and Stripes in a stiff crumple
   because it would not fall), the very
Russianness of the bear hugs was
   dizzily universal: for who
knows how to signal anything
   new without a ritual?

   Not the kitchen-table
   reader (child of the Cold War,
   of 3 x 5 cards, carbon copies,
and the manila folder), who takes a pair
   of scissors—as we do when the size
of some idea surprises—and clips
   this one into a rectangle
much like her piece of toast. There:
   it's saved, to think of later.
Yet it would be unfair
   to leave her looking smug; barely
a teenager when she watched, on
   her snowy TV screen, a man
seeming to walk on the moon, she's
   learned that some detail—

Virtual Reality or email,
　　something inexplicable and
　　unnatural—is always cropping up
for incorporation in what's human.
　　What ought to make it manageable,
and doesn't quite, is the thought
　　of humans devising it. She'll
remember Norman Thagard in June,
　　when the *Mir* (meaning Peace: but how
imagine this without agitation?)
　　docks with the *Atlantis* (meaning
the island Plato mentioned first
　　and which, like him, did not disappear
without a splash), to shuttle
　　the traveler back home—or

　　to whatever Earth has become.

FROM

Open Shutters

(2003)

TROMPE L'OEIL

All over Genoa
you see them: windows with open shutters.
Then the illusion shatters.

But that's not true. You knew
the shutters were merely painted on.
You knew it time and again.

The claim of the painted shutter
that it ever shuts the eye
of the window is an open lie.

You find its shadow-latches strike
the wall at a single angle,
like the stuck hands of a clock.

Who needs to be correct
more often than once a day?
Who needs real shadow more than play?

Inside the house, an endless
supply of clothes to wash.
On an outer wall it's fresh

paint hung out to dry—
shirttails flapping on a frieze
unruffled by any breeze,

like the words pinned to this line.
And the foreign word is a lie:
that second *l* in *l'oeil*

which only looks like an *l*, and is silent.

THE ACCORDIONIST

A whining chord of warning—the Métro's version
of Concert A—and we clear the sliding doors.
People take their seats as if assigned.
Some of them open paperbacks, like playbills,
with a formal air of expecting interruption.
Or as if the passengers themselves are actors
in a scene the stage directions might have called
Passengers reading, so that it scarcely matters
when they turn the page, or even if it's blank.

Enter a gypsy boy, who lurches forward
carrying an accordion, like a stagehand
awaiting orders where to set it down.
But when the doors wheeze shut, as if by reflex
his accordion too collapses, opens, closes
to the tune of "La Vie en Rose." He has no shoes.
Unlike the rest of us, dressed soberly
in solid colors, he's a brazen mess
of hand-me-down, ill-fitting plaids and paisleys.
He's barely old enough to be skipping school,
but no note of fear or shyness, or of shame,
shadows his face: it was years ago already
somebody taught him how to do this.

To entertain, that is—and in the coin
of the culture: an Edith Piaf song pumped
for all it's worth from the heartsore instrument
the audience links with soundtracks of old films,
as a loving camera climbs the Eiffel Tower.
But nobody is looking entertained.
They seem to be in some other kind of movie,
more modern calling for unblinking eyes

(the actor's oldest trick for coaxing tears)
that no longer lead to tears. No words. Just chords
too grand to be specified. Or is it that?
Blank faces, maybe, standing in for blank
faces, much like wearing basic black.

The boy's still young enough he plays right through
the next stop—when he might have passed a cup—
and now, with a shrug, he segues crudely to
another chestnut: "Je Ne Regrette Rien."
My station's coming up. I start to rummage
furtively in my wallet, held as close
to heart as a hand of cards (of credit cards
luck dealt me); isolate a franc. And stand,
nearly tumbling into him, to drop
the object of my keen deliberation
into the filthy pocket of his jacket,
careful not to touch it. In a second
I stride out from the car to my next scene
on the platform, where I know to exit right
and up the stairs, out to the world of light.
I'll never see him again.

But some instinct (as the train accelerates
and howls into the tunnel on its pleated
rubber joints, one huge accordion)
tells me to look back—a backward take
on Orpheus, perhaps, in which now only
Eurydice goes free? And fleetingly
I catch through windows of the next three cars
the boy repeated. No, these are his brothers—
each with an accordion in hand

and each boy inches taller than the last—
who handed down to him these blurring clothes,
and yet because the train unreels as fast
as a movie, a single window to a frame,
my eye's confused, has fused them as one boy
growing unnaturally, an understudy
condemned to play forever underground.

THE READER

It was the morning after the hundredth birthday
of Geraldine—still quite in her right mind,
a redhead now and (people said) still pretty—
who hadn't wanted a party.

Well, if she'd lost that one, she'd stood her ground
on no singing of Happy Birthday, and no cake;
next year, with any luck, they'd learn their lesson
and not be coming back.

My friend who tells the story (a distant cousin
and a favorite, allowed to spend that night
in the nursery of the Philadelphia mansion
Geraldine was born in),

woke to the wide-eyed faces of porcelain dolls
and descended a polished winding stair that led
like a dream into the sunroom, where Geraldine
sat with the paper and read.

—Or sat with the paper lifted in her hands
like the reins of Lazarus, her long-dead horse
that had jumped a thousand hurdles; shook it once
to iron out the creases;

and kept it elevated, having been
blind for the twenty years white-uniformed,
black-skinned Edwina has been paid to stand
behind her, reading the news aloud.

TWA 800

Months after it had plummeted off the coast
    of Long Island, and teams of divers scoured
the ocean floor for blasted puzzle pieces
    to hoist and reassemble like
a dinosaur (all human cargo lost,
        too shattered to restore to more
            than names), I heard my postcard

to friends in France had been delivered at last.
    Slipped in a padded bag, with a letter
from the U.S. Postal Service ("apologies
    for any inconvenience caused
by the accident"), and sea-soaked but intact,
        it was legible in every word
            I'd written ("Looking forward

to seeing you!") and on the stamp I'd pressed
    into a corner: "Harriet Quimby,
Pioneer Pilot." Under her goggled helmet,
    she was smiling like a hostess at
this fifty-cent anecdote, in which the most
        expendable is preserved and no
            rope's thrown to the rest.

ERASERS

As punishment, my father said, the nuns
   would send him and the others
out to the schoolyard with the day's erasers.

Punishment? The pounding symphony
   of padded cymbals clapped
together at arm's length overhead

(a snow of vanished alphabets and numbers
   powdering their noses
until they sneezed and laughed out loud at last)

was more than remedy, it was reward
   for all the hours they'd sat
without a word (except for passing notes)

and straight (or near enough) in front of starched
   black-and-white Sister Martha,
like a conductor raising high her chalk

baton, the only one who got to talk.
   Whatever did she teach them?
And what became of all those other boys,

poor sinners, who had made a joyful noise?
   My father likes to think,
at seventy-five, not of the white-on-black

chalkboard from whose crumbled negative
   those days were never printed,
but of word-clouds where unrecorded voices

gladly forgot themselves. And that he still
    can say so, though all the lessons,
most of the names, and (he doesn't spell

this out) it must be half the boys themselves,
    who grew up and dispersed
as soldiers, husbands, fathers, now are dust.

HARE

At odd times, harum-scarum,
after we haven't seen him
    for a week or so, he hops
    from the bushes at stage right
onto our green proscenium.

    Why do I say it's ours?
At best, I'm just a warden,
    standing with hands in suds
    at the kitchen window when
he breaks out of his warren.

    Jittery, hunted vagrant,
he leaps as fast as Aesop
    claimed his kind could leap,
    then stops still in the grass
merely because it's fragrant—

    a wholly interested,
systematic sensualist,
    a silent, smooth lawn mower
    that hardly can go slower.
Sometimes he gets ahead

    (or tries to) with the jet set,
in a long line at the airport
    pulling his legs behind him
    like luggage, bit by bit—
the nametag of his scut

attached at the last minute.
Meanwhile, I stay put
    inside the house we bought
    a year ago, a new
woman at the window—

    but of that he has no clue,
now pawn, now skipping knight
    on sun-squares on the lawn,
    while dreaming the old dream
a hare has, of his harem.

    Is he in fact the same
animal all the time?
    In my way promiscuous
    as he, how could I swear
he's not some other hare

    that pauses blank-eyed, poses
as if for praise, and then,
    rather than jump over,
inserts himself within
    a low bush, like a lover?

    Both of us bad at faces,
mere samples of our species,
    will either of us be missed?
    The dishes in my hands
are shards for the archeologist.

IN THE GUESTHOUSE

1. *Long Exposure, 1892*
All of them dead by now, and posed
so stiffly, in their sepia Sunday
best, they seem half-dead already.
Father and Eldest Son, each dressed
in high-cut jacket and floppy tie,
never get to sit in the sitting room.
They stand to face a firing squad
behind Mother and the little girls—
themselves bolt upright on the sofa,
hands at their sides, their center-parted
hair pulled back, two rows of rickrack
flanking the twenty buttons down
the plumb line of their bodices.

And here, discovered alone downstage
and slightly to the left, the boy—
such a beautiful boy. Although
they've tried to make him a little man,
upholstering him in herringbone,
you can see him itching to run out
with his hoop and stick, happy because
even at this moment, when
nobody could be happy, he knows—
in the tilt of his blond head, the frank
time-burning gaze beneath his cowlick—
that he is the most loved.

2. *Flappers, 1925*
I'm in the guesthouse some days before
focusing on another portrait:
professional, black-and-white, composed

to lend a spacious dignity
to the one life lived behind each face.
Again, the date's approximate;

I'm guessing from the arty look,
the Flapperish, drop-waisted frock
and ropes of wooden beads on the wife

of—yes, it has to be. No more
the poster boy for posterity,
he's a commanding forty. The cowlick's

still there (although now he slicks
it down with something), and he still
cocks his head to one side, a hint

of flirtation, exasperation—what?—
in the eyes he trains at the camera
as if he'd give me what I want

if only he could emerge now from
the frame. We stare in mutual
boldness while his wife's long profile

is tendered to the child between them.
One girl: a modern family.
I speculate a little son

was lost to the great flu; even so,
this fair-haired Zelda in a bob,
ten years old, would come to seem

enough, the image of her father.
The smile high-cheeked and confident,
the shining eyes, the upturned chin—

people matter more now; they'll die
less often, now that the Great War's over;
everyone's allowed to sit down.

3. *Wheelchair*, 2000
The jumbles of grinning faces jammed
together at birthdays and Christmases
in color photos around the house
    don't interest me.

They're merely *today*, or close enough;
anybody can record it
and does; if everything's recorded
    nothing is.

But puttering about, the guest
of a ghost I now am half in love with,
I'm drawn one day to pluck one image
    off the piano.

A wedding. Or some minutes after,
outside a church I've seen in town.
The bride, who has exercised her right
   to veil, white gown,

and any decorum life affords
these days, is surrounded by the girls—
some floral aunts, a gawky niece
   in her first pearls—

and all the men in blazers, khakis . . .
running shoes? Boys will be boys.
Squirming, they squint into the sun:
   some amateur

shutterbug has made sure they can't
see us, or we see them, and yet
I understand now who is shaded
   there in the wheelchair.

Dwindled, elderly, it's Zelda—
her lumpy little body slumped
like a doll's in a high chair, shoes just
   grazing the footrest.

It must be she. However many
lives her hair went through—Forties
complications held with tortoise-
   shell combs; beehives;

softer bouffants like Jackie's; fried
and sprayed gray-pincurl granny perms—
in all the years (say, seventy-five?)
    since I last saw her,

she's come back to that sleek, side-parted
bob, which (though it's white) encloses
the girl who's smiling, pert, high-cheeked,
    despite the pull

of gravity: just like her father.
Or as he was. *When did he die,
and how? What was his name? What's yours?*
    I could find out,

surely, when I leave here; the owner
might well be her granddaughter.
I could scout, too, for snapshots even
    more recent—some

get-together with no wheelchair—
to prove what I'm sensing: Zelda's gone.
Why would they think to frame this scene,
    unless it's the last?

But why should *we* care so for people
not us or ours—recognized by sight
alone—whose voices never spoke
    with wit or comfort

to us, and whose very thoughts,
imagined, every year grow quainter?
Yet they must have felt this tug as well,
    repeatedly

peering at someone they were bound
to come back to, as in a mirror.
Who says they're more anonymous
    than I am,

packing up after my two weeks
in the guesthouse? I make one last study
of Zelda's father, lingering with
    the boy, the man,

sealing his developing
face in myself for safekeeping.
Too soon to leave. But then, nobody
    ever stays here long.

DELIVERIES ONLY

for Sarah Marjorie Lyon, born in a service elevator

Your whole life long, you'll dine
out on the same questions:
In your building? On what floor?
Was it going up or down?

They'll need the precise location—
Seventy-ninth and Lex?—
as if learning it could shield them
from the consequences of sex.

Wasn't your mother a doctor?
Didn't she talk him through
how to do it? And then you'll tell them
how your father delivered you,

that only after your birth
did he think to reach in her bag
and dial 911.
He held you up like a phone

and was taught how to cut the cord.
What about proper hygiene?
When did the ambulance come?
Waiting, you were the siren,

squalling in a rage
behind the old-fashioned mesh
of the elevator door:
a Lyon cub in her cage.

Didn't your parents worry?
Hadn't they done Lamaze?
But you'll only shrug at your story:
That was the way it was.

A MORRIS DANCE

Across the Common, on a lovely May
day in New England, I see and hear
the Middle Ages drawing near,
bells tinkling, pennants bright and gay—
    a parade of Morris dancers.

One plucks a lute. One twirls a cape.
Up close, a lifted pinafore
exposes cellulite, and more.
O why aren't they in better shape,
    the middle-aged Morris dancers?

Already it's not hard to guess
their treasurer—her; their president—him;
the Wednesday night meetings at the gym.
They ought to practice more, or less,
    the middle-aged Morris dancers.

Short-winded troubadours and pages,
milkmaids with osteoporosis—
what really makes me so morose is
how they can't admit their ages,
    the middle-aged Morris dancers.

Watching them gamboling and tripping
on Maypole ribbons like leashed dogs,
then landing, thunderously, on clogs,
I have to say I feel like skipping
    the middle-aged Morris dancers.

Yet bunions and receding gums
have humbled me; I know my station
as a member of their generation.
Maybe they'd let me play the drums,
   the middle-aged Morris dancers.

ANOTHER SESSION

I.
You opened with the rules. Outside this room
nothing I said inside would be repeated
unless in your best judgment I posed harm
to myself or others. It was like being read
my rights in some film noir—but I was glad
already I'd at last turned myself in,
guilty of anxiety and depression.

And worse. Confess it: worse. Of narcissist
indifference to how other people felt.
Railing against myself, making a list
of everything (I thought), I'd left a fault
unturned: the one of needing to be praised
for forcing these indictments from my throat.
For saying them well. For speaking as I wrote.

2.
Not that the goal was chalking up demerits.
Indeed, I hoped you were basically on my side.
That's how I interpreted your nod,
your pleasant face (at first, a little hard
to judge behind that beard), your intelligent
air of listening further than I meant.
And never falsely, just to raise my spirits,
but because you couldn't not be interested.

"You writers!" When the outburst came, I started
out of my chair. (I'd had a habit then—
feet on your coffee table. Never again.)
"This is real life. You don't live in a novel.
People aren't characters. They're not a symbol."
We stared, stunned at the other, stony-hearted.

3.
Once or twice a week, for a year. But ten
years ago already, so that today
those intimate, subtle, freeform sessions shrink
to memorized refrains: "You seem to think
people can read your mind. You have to *say*"—
itself said kindly—or that time you accused me
of picturing love too much like "Barbie and Ken.
Why does it have to be all youth and beauty?"

Therapists have themes, as writers do.
(A few of mine, then: the repertoire includes
clocks, hands, untimely death, snow-swollen clouds.)
Like it or not, I picked up more from you:
No showing off. In failure, no surprise.
Gratitude. Trust. Forgiveness. Fantasies.

4.

The last time I saw your face—how far back now?—
was when I took my daughters (I still don't
know what possessed me) to a "family restaurant."
Dinosaur portions, butter enough to drown
all sorrows in, cakes melded from candy bars . . .
Having filed you away for years and years,
suddenly I was nervous, my life on show.
I'm still married, thanks. Husband's out of town.

But there was no talking to you across the aisle
where, by some predestined trick of seating,
your brood in its entirety was eating
(their dinners, I suppose, were just as vile)
with backs to me, remaining as they must
faceless to patients even from the past.

5.

Killed instantly. That's what a mutual friend
told me when I asked how it had happened.
Good, I said, *I'm glad he didn't suffer—*
each of us reaching (not far) for a phrase
from a lifetime stock of journalists' clichés
which, we had learned, provide a saving buffer
within our bifurcated selves: the one
that's horrified; the one that must go on.

Killed in a bicycle race. I've scrapped the Wheel
of Fortune, the Road of Life. No, this is real,
there's no script to consult: you've lost your body.
Still having one, I pace, I stretch, I cough,
I wash my face. But then I'm never ready.
This is the sonnet I've been putting off.

6.
And also this one, in which your fancy bike
hits a concrete barrier and you fly
over it into fast *oncoming traffic*—
the obituary's formula for one man
driving a truck, who didn't even have
time to believe the corner of his eye,
until the thing was done, and he must live
always as if this nightmare were the one
deed he was born to do and to relive,
precisely the sort of person you would trust
in fifty-minute sessions to forgive
himself, to give himself at least two years
of post-traumatic whatsit to adjust
to thoughts of all those people left in tears.

7.
Only once did you confide a story
from your own life. (And only to illustrate
how long "people" take to overcome a shock.)
An accident—you broke your neck? Your back?
Shameful I don't remember—and for three
years you'd take a detour to avoid
the sight of it: that swinging, high red light
somebody ran, that road that crossed a road.

A run-through of the sped-up, drawn-out second
of terror before your second, actual end.
Swinging past the turnoff to your clinic
today, I saw I'd never choose to drive
that street again; would steer around the panic
rather than fail to find you there alive.

8.
Notice—but you can't—I don't write your name.
People aren't characters. Here's my concession
(small) to that view, and your need of privacy
which, I suspect, went beyond your profession.
When I knew you—no, you knew *me*—I'd missed the easy
truth we had acquaintances in common.
(A good thing, probably, I'd been too dim
to ask you; you too classy to let on.)

Nor did I find the public facts in print
(*age 53, father of three, an active
member of his church*) until you'd long
been dead. That July I came and went.
You reached me in a place I don't belong—
seventeen months later, Christmas Eve.

9.
I'd got there early, casually saved a front
pew for the whole family with some flung
mittens and hats. (In gestures we assume
the shoulder-to-shoulder permanence of home.)
Shouldn't we come more often? "The Power of Love":
our sermon. A list called "Flowers in Memory of"
on the program's final page. I was feeling faint.
Your name. Your father's name? Something was wrong.

I knew it was you. The church was going black.
Head down: my first anxiety attack
since the bad old days. Your face at the restaurant.
My plate heaped up with food I didn't want.
Keep the head down. People would be saying
to themselves (and close enough) that I was praying.

10.

Revise our last encounter. I'd rather say
it was that day a decade ago we made
a formal farewell: I was going away
on a long trip. If I needed you, I said,
when I got back, I'd be sure to give a call.
You stood up, and I finally saw how tall
you were; I'd never registered how fit.
Well, all we'd done for a year was talk and sit.

Paris, you said. Then, awkwardly, *Lucky you.*
Possessor of my secrets, not a friend,
colder, closer, our link unbreakable.
Yet we parted better than people often do.
We looked straight at each other. Was that a smile?
I thanked you for everything. You shook my hand.

MIDSUMMER, GEORGIA AVENUE

Happiness: a high, wide porch, white columns
crowned by the crepe-paper party hats
of hibiscus; a rocking chair; iced tea; a book;
an afternoon in late July to read it,
or read the middle of it, having leisure
to mark the place and enter it tomorrow
just as you left it (knock-knock of woodpecker
keeping yesterday's time, cicada's buzz,
the turning of another page, and somewhere
a question raised and dropped, the pendulum-
swing of a wind chime). Back and forth, the rocker
and the reading eye, and isn't half

your jittery, odd joy the looking out
now and again across the road to where,
under the lush allées of long-lived trees
conferring shade and breeze on those who feel
none of it, a hundred stories stand confined,
each to their single page of stone? Not far,
the distance between you and them: a breath,
a heartbeat dropped, a word in your two-faced
book that invites you to its party only
to sadden you when it's over. And so you stay
on your teetering perch, you move and go nowhere,
gazing past the heat-struck street that's split

down the middle—not to put too fine
a point on it—by a double yellow line.

FOR EMILY AT FIFTEEN

Sirens living in silence, why would they leave the sea?

—EMILY LEITHAUSER

Allow me one more try,
though you and I both know
you're too old now to need
writing about by me—

you who composed a sonnet
and enclosed it in a letter,
casually, with family news,
while I was away;

who rummaged in convention's
midden for tools and symbols
and made with them a maiden
voyage from mere verse

into the unmapped world
of poetry. A mermaid
(like Eve, you wrote—a good
analogy, and yet

your creature acts alone)
chooses to rise from wordless
unmindful happiness
up to the babbling surface

of paradox and pain.
I whose job it's been
to protect you read my lesson:
you'll wriggle from protection.

Half-human and half-fish
of adolescence, take
my compliments, meant half
as from a mother, half

one writer to another,
for rhymes in which you bury
ironies—for instance,
sirens into *silence;*

and since I've glimpsed a shadow,
forgive how glad I felt
when I set down your sonnet
to read your letter again

with only silliness in it,
the old tenth-grade bravado:
"Oh well, I bombed the chem test.
Latin's a yawn a minute."

PEONIES

Heart-transplants my friend handed me:
four of her own peony bushes
in their fall disguise, the arteries
of truncated, dead wood protruding
from clumps of soil fine-veined with worms.

"Better get them in before the frost."
And so I did, forgetting them
until their June explosion when
it seemed at once they'd fallen in love,
had grown two dozen pink hearts each.

Extravagance, exaggeration,
each one a girl on her first date,
excess perfume, her dress too ruffled,
the words he spoke to her too sweet—
but he was young; he meant it all.

And when they could not bear the pretty
weight of so much heart, I snipped
their dew-sopped blooms; stuffed them in vases
in every room like tissue-boxes
already teary with self-pity.

AFTER SEPTEMBER

Evening, four weeks later.
The next jet from the nearby Air Force base
repeats its shuddering exercise
closer and closer overhead.
A full moon lifts again in the fragile sky,
with every minute taking on
more light from the grounded sun, until
it's bright enough to read the reported
facts of this morning's paper by—
finally, a moon that glows
so brilliantly it might persuade us
that out there *somebody knows.*

A comfort once—the omniscience
of Mother, Father, TV, moon.
Later, in the long afternoon
of adolescence, I lay on the grass
and philosophized with a friend:
would we choose to learn our death date
(some eighty years from now, of course)?
Did it exist yet? And if so,
did we believe in fate?
(What *we* thought: to the growing
narcissist, that was the thing to know.)
Above our heads, the clouds kept drifting,
uncountable, unrecountable,
like a dreamer's game of chess
in which, it seemed, one hand alone
moved all the pieces, all of them white,

and in the hand they changed
liquidly and at once into
shapes we almost—no,
we couldn't name.

But if there were one force
greater than we, had I ever really
doubted that he or she
or it would be literate?
Would see into the world's own heart?
To know all is to forgive all—
(now, where had I read that?).
Evil would be the opposite, yes?—
scattershot and obtuse:
what hates you, what you hate
hidden in cockpits, caves, motel rooms;
too many of them to love
or, anyway, too late.
By now I've raided thousands
of stories in the paper for
thinkable categories:
unlettered schoolboys with one Book
learned by heresy and hearsay;
girls never sent to school;
men's eyes fixed on the cause;
living women draped in shrouds,
eyes behind prison-grilles of gauze.

Mine, behind reading glasses
(updated yearly, to lend no greater
clarity than the illusion
that one can stay in place),

look up and guess what the moon
means by its blurred expression.
Something to do with grief
that grief now seems old-fashioned—
a gesture that the past
gave the past for being lost—
and that the future is newly lost
to an unfocused dread
of what may never happen
and nobody can stop.

Not tired yet, wound-up, almost
too glad to be alive—as if
this too were dangerous—
I imagine the synchronized operations
across the neighborhood:
putting the children to bed;
laying out clean clothes;
checking that the clock radio
is set for six o'clock tomorrow,
to alarm ourselves with news.

Acknowledgments

I am deeply grateful to the Bogliasco Foundation and to The MacDowell Colony for residencies which enabled me to write many of these poems. Thanks also to the editors of the publications where the following new poems first appeared, sometimes in slightly different form.

"Lunar Eclipse" and "Somebody Else's Baby" in *New Letters*
"Somebody Else's Baby" reprinted by Ted Kooser in his syndicated
    newspaper column, "American Life in Poetry"
"Aurora Borealis" and "Musical Chair" in *RSA* (*Rivista di Studi Nord
    Americani*); reprinted in *New Letters*
"Wake-up Call" in *RSA*; reprinted in *Mare Nostrum*
"Costanza Bonarelli" in *The American Scholar*; reprinted in *The Best
    American Poems* 2005 and in *Mare Nostrum*
"Point of View" in *The New Republic*
"Beach House, Space-Time" in *Vintage: Ten Years of the Mildura Writ-
    ers' Festival*
"Friday Harbor, 10 A.M." in *The New Yorker*
"A Phone Call to the Future" in *The Georgia Review*; reprinted in *The
    Best American Poems* 2006
"Picket Fence with Peacock" in *The Los Angeles Review*
"Song of the Children" in *Poetry Northwest*

"Geraniums Before Blue Mountain" and "Please Forward" in *The Hopkins Review*

"Executive Shoeshine" in *The Atlantic Monthly*

"Wake-up Call" is dedicated to Massimo Bacigalupo; "Friday Harbor, 10 A.M." to Richard Kenney and Carol Light; "Lunar Eclipse" to the memory of Anthony Hecht, and to Helen Hecht; "Costanza Bonarelli" to Wendy Watson and John Varriano; "Song of the Children" to Colette and James Rossant; "Beach House, Space-Time" to Cynthia Zarin and Joseph Goddu; "Point of View" to Heather McHugh; "Goodbye, Train" to Nancy Doherty; "Musical Chair" to Rose Ruze; "Executive Shoeshine" to Madeleine Blais; "Picket Fence with Peacock" to Stephen Yenser; "Poetry Slalom" to Peggy O'Brien; "Roses and Mona Lisa" to Peggy O'Shea; "Aurora Borealis" to North Cairn; "Please Forward" to David Schweizer; "Somebody Else's Baby" to Brad Leithauser; and "A Phone Call to the Future" to Emily and Hilary Leithauser.

A NOTE ABOUT THE AUTHOR

Mary Jo Salter was born in Grand Rapids, Michigan, and grew up in Detroit and Baltimore. She was educated at Harvard and Cambridge and worked as a staff editor at *The Atlantic Monthly* and as poetry editor of *The New Republic*. She is also a coeditor of *The Norton Anthology of Poetry*. In addition to her five previous poetry collections, she is the author of a children's book, *The Moon Comes Home,* and is a playwright and lyricist. After many years of teaching at Mount Holyoke College, she is now Professor in The Writing Seminars at Johns Hopkins University. She and her husband, the writer Brad Leithauser, divide their time between Amherst, Massachusetts, and Baltimore.

A NOTE ON THE TYPE

This book was set in Fairfield, the first typeface from the hand of the distinguished American artist and engraver Rudolph Ruzicka (1883–1978). In its structure Fairfield displays the sober and sane qualities of the master craftsman whose talent has long been dedicated to clarity. It is this trait that accounts for the trim grace and vigor, the spirited design and sensitive balance, of this original typeface.

Rudoph Ruzicka was born in Bohemia and came to America in 1894. He set up his own shop, devoted to wood engraving and printing, in New York in 1913 after a varied career working as a wood engraver, in photoengraving and banknote printing plants, and as an art director and freelance artist. He designed and illustrated many books, and was the creator of a considerable list of individual prints—wood engravings, line engravings on copper, and aquatints.

Composed by Creative Graphics,
Allentown, Pennsylvania

Printed and bound by R. R. Donnelley,
Harrisonburg, Virginia

Designed by Soonyoung Kwon